Once Upon A Dream

Little Laureates

Edited By Lynsey Evans

First published in Great Britain in 2024 by:

YoungWriters
Est. 1991

Young Writers
Remus House
Coltsfoot Drive
Peterborough
PE2 9BF
Telephone: 01733 890066
Website: www.youngwriters.co.uk

All Rights Reserved
Book Design by Ashley Janson
© Copyright Contributors 2024
Softback ISBN 978-1-83565-451-4
Printed and bound in the UK by BookPrintingUK
Website: www.bookprintinguk.com
YB0591A

FOREWORD

Welcome Reader, to a world of dreams.

For Young Writers' latest competition, we asked our writers to dig deep into their imagination and create a poem that paints a picture of what they dream of, whether it's a make-believe world full of wonder or their aspirations for the future.

The result is this collection of fantastic poetic verse that covers a whole host of different topics. Let your mind fly away with the fairies to explore the sweet joy of candy lands, join in with a game of fantasy football, or you may even catch a glimpse of a unicorn or another mythical creature. Beware though, because even dreamland has dark corners, so you may turn a page and walk into a nightmare!

Whereas the majority of our writers chose to stick to a free verse style, others gave themselves the challenge of other techniques such as acrostics and rhyming couplets.

Each piece in this collection shows the writers' dedication and imagination – we truly believe that seeing their work in print gives them a well-deserved boost of pride, and inspires them to keep writing, so we hope to see more of their work in the future!

CONTENTS

Craighead Primary School, Glasgow

Maya McLaughlin (8)	1
Cooper McIlvenna (8)	2
Harris Cunningham (8)	3
Aidan Marshall (8)	4
Ella McColl (8)	5
Lewis Robertson (8)	6
Rex McCaffer (8)	7
Noah Irvine (8)	8
Amélia Serra (8)	9
Harris Blackburn (8)	10
Paul Ball (8)	11
Blake Cameron (8)	12
Zack Steele (8)	13
Maisie Bouse (8)	14
Sophie Syme (8)	15
Eva Noble (9)	16
Emma Macphail (8)	17
Louisa McCluskey (8)	18
Arran Anderson (8)	19
Alice Kinnear (8)	20
Freddie Barbour (8)	21
Esther Moody (8)	22
Jayden Butler (8)	23
Harris Anderson (8)	24
Kai Prentice (8)	25
Archie Robertson (8)	26
Archie Quinn (8)	27

Gilbert Inglefield Academy, Leighton Buzzard

Michael O'Callaghan (10)	28
Sophia Snee (11)	30
Sienna Keating (10)	32
Rosie Siddon (10)	33
Bethany Field (11)	34
Amelia Oake (11)	35
Lucie Jones (10)	36
Penelope Carter (11)	37
Oscar Adlem (10)	38
Jasmine Martell (10)	39
Harrison Reyland (11)	40
Monty Wisdom (11)	42
Julian Kildusis (11)	44
Lauren Booth (10)	45
Keavy Flynn (10)	46
Zac Lee (10)	47
Mellisa Afram (11)	48
Daniel McShane (10)	49
Isla Croft (10)	50
Daisy Mowbray (10)	51
Deon Santo (10)	52
Samuel Lambert (11)	53
Evie Reynolds (11)	54
Owen Gould (10)	55
Daisy O'Shea (11)	56
Summer Archer Baker (10)	57
Aidija Selukaite (11)	58
Sam Ferguson (11)	59
Casey Reed	60
Alice Robertson-Hills (11)	61
Lewis Payne (11)	62
Mason Hollingsworth (11)	63
Max Bellamy (10)	64

Maggie Grimes (11)	65
April Lemon (11)	66
Thomas Millett (11)	67
Nicole Botez (10)	68
Theo Rye (11)	69
Hannah Booth (10)	70
Tommy Ogden (10)	71
Rose Whatman (10)	72
Cody Francis (10)	73
Tiana Chase (11)	74
Jake Bromley (10)	75
Isabella Higgins (11)	76
Ava-Rose Barry (11)	77
Jamie Fletcher (11)	78
Ronnie Millson (11)	79
Xavier Procter (11)	80

Heyford Park School, Upper Heyford

Seth Wright (10)	81
Willow Steele (10)	82
Dasha Bochkala (10)	84
Charlotte Waton (9)	85
Ivana Simakoski (9)	86
Lucas Bird (9)	87
Dylan Pugh (9)	88
Juniper Zeyfert (10)	89
Georgia Bichard (10)	90
Lea Smit (9)	91
Jack Laker (10)	92
Jessica Luciano (9)	93
Rhys Viglieno (10)	94
Jane Keenan (10)	95

Kirkpatrick Fleming Primary School, Lockerbie

Sadie Muir (9)	96
Lilly Woodward (9)	97
Clara Little (9)	98
Sophia Shields (9)	99
Elsie McCracken (9)	100
Vilte Narbutaite (8)	101

Finlay Wylie (9)	102
Lily Rae (9)	103
Eddie Woodward (9)	104
Eidigh Davidson (8)	105
Jack Balmer (9)	106
Cooper Richardson (8)	107
Isabella Thomson (8)	108
Wills Halliday (9)	109
Joseph Graham (9)	110
Alice Ewings (8)	111
Jack Haillday (9)	112
Louie Johnston (9)	113
Jasmine Murray (9)	114
Sam Rae (8)	115
Soren Corkill (8)	116
Harley-J Ayres (8)	117

Our Lady Of Lourdes RC Primary School, Bolton

Kara Corkill (9)	118
Antoni Joseph (8)	120
Darlene Acheampong (9)	121
Isla Barnes (9)	122
Daniel Shennowo (8)	123
Ruby Smalley (8)	124
Amina Khan (8)	125
Jack Porter (8)	126
Poppy Nesbitt (8)	127
George Taylor (9)	128
Holly Carberry (9)	129
Molly Newns (9)	130
Leander Sakala (8)	131
Gabriel Cullis (8)	132
Lorenza Grae Lopez (8)	133
Grayson Booker-Bryon (8)	134
Ollie Haslam (9)	135
Elliott Leach (8)	136
Jacob Smally (8)	137
Clara O'Brien (9)	138
Rosalie Parkinson (9)	139
Aham Zubair (8)	140
Archie Earp (8)	141

St Peter's Catholic Primary School, Waterlooville

Ava Tooes (10)	142
Isla Jordan (9)	144
Bella Champion (10)	145
Amelia Knight (10)	146
Eve Jordan (9)	148
Bethany Stockman (9)	150
Alexander Broadway (10)	151
Temperance Parkes (10)	152
Sophia Lipscomb (10)	153
Molly Nelson (9)	154
Makayla Williams (10)	155
Florence Turner (9)	156
Catherine Cope (9)	157
Taylor Barnfield (9)	158
Fia Panamchickal (9)	159
Hallie Puddick (10)	160
Maisie Hillier (10)	161
Caitlin Nibigira (9)	162

St Winefride's Catholic Primary School, Shepshed

Kaydan Holland (11)	163
Isaac Wasilewski (10)	164
Eric Turland (10)	166
Freya Dunmore (11)	168
Henry Clarke (10)	170
Jinu Labadia (11)	172
Evan Saunders (10)	173
Hannah Sherwood (10)	174
Fergus Flynne (11)	175
Mabel Hill (10)	176
Yami Ugorji (10)	178
Nancie Robinson (11)	179
Clara Wardle (10)	180
Zara Bayley (11)	181
Daisy Wright (10)	182
Casey Clare (11)	183
Coco-Marley Gray (11)	184
Joshua Monk (11)	185
Lucas Routledge (10)	186
Evie Llewelyn (10)	187
Lerell Williams-Farmer (11)	188
Oscar Johnson (11)	189

Stoneydown Park Primary School, London

Eva Kisyora (11) & Samantha	190
Jamie Bertram (10)	193
Jasmia Lillie Kaur Marsh (9)	194
Una Miller (9)	196
Arianna Laskou Fabrizi (11)	198
Ruby Swift (10)	200
Alex Jeffery (8)	201
Aleen Suleman (11)	202
Arsema Yohhannes (10)	203
Juno Scaife Duff (10)	204
Lola Theophanous Richards (10)	205
Hareem Shazad (10)	206
Delia Danciu (10)	207
Robin Coffey (10)	208
Leo Michael Hoyle Buryy (8)	209
Eila Danaher (11)	210
Teddy Buryy (9)	211
Zoë McClintock (8)	212
Soner Ramadan (9)	213
Alisia Blaiu (11) & Lena Bak (11)	214
Roisin McTernan (10)	215
Iris Hobhouse (7)	216
Nell Dyer (10)	217
Janae Benjamin (10)	218
Fatima Sherazaye (7)	219
Macy Matthews (10)	220
Irene Mara Arroyo-Kalin (8)	221
Lara Hodgkin (7)	222
Flynn Bullett (7)	223
Dylan Junhua Lim (8)	224
Charlotte Lawrence (9)	225
Rose Gulla Martinelli-Kinmonth (7)	226
Abel Shajahan (8)	227
Ania Jenkins (11) & Nina Dall'Igna Kennedy (11)	228
Elisa Parker (8)	229
Isaac Knowles (9)	230

Murphy Hyland (8)	231
Lily Kidby (9)	232
Olivia Henrichfreise (8)	233
Lena Bak (10)	234
Mae Milner-Feliho (10)	235
Yaswinthan Pirabakaran (7)	236
Amelie Dhoot (9)	237
Isabella-Naomi Olohigam Ochinyabo (8) & Naomi Elizabeth Eisenstein (10)	238
	239
Elspeth Simonds-Gooding (8)	240
Nathaniel Kyeremeh Peprah (11)	241
Dylan Roe (8)	242
Griffith Kingwell (10)	243
Jaiyan Harrie Marsh (8)	244
Olive Bowyer (8)	245
Zara O'Neill (9) & Nina Hobhouse (9)	246
Lennie Bradley (9)	247
Iris Simonds-Gooding (10)	248
Ivan Kennedy (9)	249

THE POEMS

The Famous Castle

F amous people can be nice
A nd I heard they live in castles
M ost of the knights sleep during the day
O n the roof, the guards stand guard
U nicorns on the hills next to the castle
S o many people want to be like the king and queen

C astles are huge and magnificent
A nd have princesses
S ome castles are on hills
T his castle is next to the ocean
L east the castle has room for me
E xcited to be in a famous castle.

Maya McLaughlin (8)
Craighead Primary School, Glasgow

Rich Car Crash

R accoons were scratching the car
I n the tigers go to scratch the car
C ontinue driving and a lion bites a bit of car
H ammerhead sharks jump at us!

C ontinue driving and monkeys appear
A pitbull dents the car
R iding my car next to a dragon.

C an't see because the dragon's fire
R un to fire water at it
A ll animals run away
S weden is our final destination
H ooray, we are safe.

Cooper McIlvenna (8)
Craighead Primary School, Glasgow

I'm A Famous Footballer

F amous footballers are cool
O verhead kicks are cool
O verhead kicks are amazing
T iny balls are nearly hard to kick
B ad footballers are getting better
A sport called football is fun
L ove to play with my friend
L earn how to play football, it's fun.

Harris Cunningham (8)
Craighead Primary School, Glasgow

Parkour

P arkour is extreme stunts
A mazing stunts can be very dangerous
R unning up the Empire State Building
K nowledge is key to staying safe
O utside is the best place to do parkour
U nbelievable parkour is very cool
R oller skates can be used for parkour.

Aidan Marshall (8)
Craighead Primary School, Glasgow

We Win The Lottery

L oving people in a loving family,
O bviously, they buy lottery tickets.
T his time they won.
T hen they got a big, big, big mansion.
E veryone is happy and shocked.
R eally big limo as well.
Y awning after a long day of being rich.

Ella McColl (8)
Craighead Primary School, Glasgow

A Boy And His Dog

B oomer is my dog.
O ne day, me and my dog were out and another dog appeared.
O nce when me and my dog were out, we saw people walking.
M ore people were walking.
E ggs were on the campsites
R accoons were running on the campsites too.

Lewis Robertson (8)
Craighead Primary School, Glasgow

Travelling The Multiverse

T and Terr are crazy on a ship
R egold Raider joined us on the ship
A liens took our ship and gave us an old ship
V ictory is coming! Let's hurry!
E veryone is chilling on the ship
L egends are the best astronauts.

Rex McCaffer (8)
Craighead Primary School, Glasgow

Spaceman

A way in a spaceship
S paceship is black
T rying to get to deep space
R eady to go
O ver to the pilot
N early there!
A bout ten hours
U nder the stars
T here are space pirates.

Noah Irvine (8)
Craighead Primary School, Glasgow

Dragons And Witches

D ragons - lots of them!
R *oar!* Witches are attacking,
A rgh! A dragon is coming,
G et it and train it,
O h, it is hurt, fix it,
N ow get revenge on the witches,
S pell on! Dragon saved.

Amélia Serra (8)
Craighead Primary School, Glasgow

Zombie Chase

Z ombies are chasing me
O ctopuses are in lava
M onster zombies are chasing me
B ehind the wall, there is a monster
I am with my dad, my brother, and my mum
E ggs are sizzling in the lava.

Harris Blackburn (8)
Craighead Primary School, Glasgow

My Friends And Me

F un playing with friends.
R unning to the trees.
I climbed up the tree.
E veryone sees me falling.
N ow I feel sore.
D reams of fun times.
S ean and Blake are the best.

Paul Ball (8)
Craighead Primary School, Glasgow

I Got Bit By A Spider

S pider Mum is big!
P lug the hoover in.
I need to catch the spider.
D ived into the cupboard.
E dge of the door, the spider spun a web.
R eady to catch the spider with the hoover.

Blake Cameron (8)
Craighead Primary School, Glasgow

The Kraken

K raken lives in the sea.
R an into the sea to fight it.
A round the corner was a hammerhead shark.
K raken got defeated.
E verybody was nearly safe,
N ow the stars were here!

Zack Steele (8)
Craighead Primary School, Glasgow

Star Saved Me

S tanding next to a cradle on a bike,
T he fairies were there as well.
A nd the wizard was there.
R ight at that moment the dragon came.
S o the fairies and the wizard helped me escape.

Maisie Bouse (8)
Craighead Primary School, Glasgow

Locked In School

S tuck in school
C onfused as it's night-time
H aving dinner in the lunch hall is so creepy
O pen the secret door
O ut pops the button
L ocked in school no more.

Sophie Syme (8)
Craighead Primary School, Glasgow

A Happy Ending

P rincess in a palace on a high hill
A lligators in ponds outside the palace
L evitate into the sky
A world of imagination
C ats and dogs
E very kind of horse.

Eva Noble (9)
Craighead Primary School, Glasgow

A Day Of A Teacher

S illy kids are being mean.
C ool kids are dancing.
H appy kids are playing.
O utdoors is fun.
O utside there are people.
L oud kids play in the room.

Emma Macphail (8)
Craighead Primary School, Glasgow

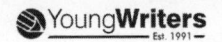

Monster House

M ad and scary
O ut of this world
N ever ends
S cary as ever
T rapped in a different dimension
E ver so long
R ats and spiders and worms.

Louisa McCluskey (8)
Craighead Primary School, Glasgow

Rich Man Robbed

R oom full of games
O pen the door of my mansion
B urglar appears on the camera
B uild a taser
E veryone runs away
D ived back into my games room.

Arran Anderson (8)
Craighead Primary School, Glasgow

Flying With Unicorns

U nicorns are nice
N early time to fly
I n unicorn world
C ool colours
O h my fairies
R eally good fairies
N early time to go home.

Alice Kinnear (8)
Craighead Primary School, Glasgow

Lost In The Forest

F orest river flowing
O ut the animals came
R ats were running
E ach animal came out one by one
S piders were climbing trees
T rees are tall.

Freddie Barbour (8)
Craighead Primary School, Glasgow

The House Of Fun

H ouse with windows
O pen the door and Maisie says, "Hi!"
U nder the staircase, a monster crawls out
S cared, we scream
E xit the house now!

Esther Moody (8)
Craighead Primary School, Glasgow

A Shadow

S hadow - big, dark and scary
H ouse is spooky
A clown jump-scares me
D isappears into the shadows
O utside I run
W here could he be...?

Jayden Butler (8)
Craighead Primary School, Glasgow

Stuck

S tars are out and it is black
T rying to get out of the field
U nder the stars
C limbing the fence, but can't get out
K eeping alive!

Harris Anderson (8)
Craighead Primary School, Glasgow

The Forest

F lying birds
O ver the trees
R esting after a long flight
E ating berries
S leeping in their nests
T rees are tall.

Kai Prentice (8)
Craighead Primary School, Glasgow

Rich Car Crash

B ob is my robot
O ne in the world
B ob is playful

C rocs on my car
A pples on my car
R ex in my car.

Archie Robertson (8)
Craighead Primary School, Glasgow

Dark House

H ouse is dark.
O ld and scary.
U gly and weird.
S ome wizard comes into the house.
E veryone is flying.

Archie Quinn (8)
Craighead Primary School, Glasgow

Fortnite

When I go to play, a sudden sight awaits,
I go through a portal, something really strange
And then me and my friends start a game!
As we skydive down through the breezy air
We find tall towers as big as Thanos, we find its Lavish Lair.
We find weapons, slurps, and barrels too (as quick as we can).

There are already kids fighting the boss, Oscar, we third-party them,
And we finish Oscar with only one shot.
Theo gets the Mythic Auto-Frenzy shotgun,
Aiden gets the medallion,
And I get the Mythic Chest in the vault.
Now, we enter the vault and loot the place,
We get Thunder Burst SMGs, which are as quick as Spider-Man, a sniper, an AR, a grapple blade and heals, which are in my inventory!

We set off on our hoverboards and we find ourselves in a 'Sweaty Build' battle. I ARed a kid, but he got me with a shotgun.
I popped a mini and both of my friends got knocked.

I went full sweat mode and I beat them up,
Then I revived my friends.

I said, "Okay, this is a one vs one situation,
And we'd better win this one!"
I sniped a kid, same as Theo,
"The last kid is distressed, let's push!"

We got the last kid and I did the Real Slim Shady.
Theo does the Griddy and Aiden Gets Schwifty,
Then we all say,
"Wenegade Waider!"

Michael O'Callaghan (10)
Gilbert Inglefield Academy, Leighton Buzzard

The Animals' Forest

I sat on my sofa,
It looked as white as snow,
I was the only one here,
I turned on the TV and clicked on a film.

As it turned on I heard a knock at the door,
It was very loud all my cats ran upstairs,
And I walked over to the coal-black door,
An old sketchy man peered into my house,
I feared him so I stepped back,
He said, "Hello little girl, want to see magic?"
"No," I replied and slammed the door.

I turned around and I was in a beautiful forest,
With fireflies and blossom trees, it was perfect.
But then I noticed all eight cats were there
(The one from my dreamland).

I walked along and everything turned grey,
Trees were dead, and mud was on the floor,
It was like there was a wall there.
The dead leaves falling,
From the trees were scaring the cats,
But the cats found a room in a tree.

And I waited for what seemed like years,
A spider crawled onto my cheek,
As we crawled out I was in my home,
Missing posters everywhere,
It had been twenty years
And that was my nightmare.

Sophia Snee (11)
Gilbert Inglefield Academy, Leighton Buzzard

The Witch's Cabin

I've heard this story before,
About a cabin, housing four.
On my walk by the glistening riverbank,
I saw through a window some weird little fish in a tank.
I found it so strange, I decided to go in...

I was running away, they were right on my trail,
Little did I know they were destined to fail.
I was nearly there, nearly at home,
But as I slowed down, I heard them starting to moan.
"Why do they run, we're not trying to kill?"
"But with all the potions and bubbles they think that we will."
"All we've wanted, all our life is a friend."
"I know but no one ever stops in the end."

At this point, I felt bad,
Because they were obviously sad.
"I've decided to be your friend."
"Huh, I guess some do stop in the end."
"Come, let us show you our cabin."

Sienna Keating (10)
Gilbert Inglefield Academy, Leighton Buzzard

The Circus Nightmare

I woke up on the cold rubbery floor,
I didn't know how I had got there, but I felt petrified.
Red balloons were squeaking together eerily and the wind seemed to scream...
"Help!"

Slowly, I got up off the floor,
I didn't know what to do, but maybe there was a door?
Suddenly my hair pricked up and I heard a faint giggling.
The giggling was like a song that would get stuck in your head.

I don't know why, but I started to run as fast as my legs would carry me.
The laughing got closer and it sounded like a maniac as I ran.
Sometimes people think of circuses as happy dreamlands, but this was definitely the opposite.
I was terrified and not looking at where I was going but then I slipped on something dark and red.
Then I felt something sharp in my head,
Then I woke up in my bed,
Screaming in my head.

Rosie Siddon (10)
Gilbert Inglefield Academy, Leighton Buzzard

Space Africa

When the shining moon rises to say morning,
All the space animals wake up yawning.
The lion roars to wake up his pride,
While stunning rainbow birds glide.

The ocean-blue rhino goes to wash his horn,
Right at the crack of dawn.
A family of little spotted deer creeps out of home,
Unaware of the stalking cheetah alone.

The golden elephants throw their trunks into the air.
A hippo referees the fight to make sure it is fair.
A seal taking shelter from a freeze,
While many dazzling animals enjoy a breeze.

Horses leaping on sparkling stars above the moon,
While pandas enjoy a bamboo tune.
Ten-legged ants get tucked into bed,
Many animals rest their heads.

And as their eyes close,
Nobody knows.
Where will their dreams take them...
It remains unknown.

Bethany Field (11)
Gilbert Inglefield Academy, Leighton Buzzard

Dream In A Dream

I had a dream I woke up in the morning
Things looked pretty boring
I heard Harry Potter snoring

I went down to eat,
There was some interesting food beneath my feet
There was gloop and glob
All over the walls
Hermione Granger was on the sofa watching TV
She had leftovers on top of her knees

I went back to bed and snored and snored
I had a dream I was a galaxy mermaid, sleeping on the stars
I saw a girl over on Mars
I was in this space full of stars

Her home was a space ball in this space
Her home was Saturn where she ate
She had a pet, a starfish to be exact
We went to her house where she ate

We went to the garden, the ring around her house
We had some fun running around and then hit the hay.

Amelia Oake (11)
Gilbert Inglefield Academy, Leighton Buzzard

The Nightmare

There once lived a girl,
With teeth as white as pearls,
She had her friends round for a sleepover,
Lilia, Teigen and Penelope.
They all went into the woods with stress weighing heavily.
It started to feel like they were losing vision
And the terrible feeling of suspicion
There was a man with a white face
With his nose that was red
And quite a fast running pace
With his messed-up head
He was trying to make them dead
They ran into the streets
Looking at the bright lights
Trying to think
How to make things right
So they ran up the hill with the forest on it
And called the police
But it was too late
He already did his kill
So now they suffer in the cold forever
Then I awake, still and let out a shrill.

Lucie Jones (10)
Gilbert Inglefield Academy, Leighton Buzzard

Stuck In The Woods

S tuck in the woods, with a fifty percent survival chance,
T eigan, me, Lucie and Sophie trek through the woods,
U nsure whether we can hear wolves or not,
C ircling the forest with nothing to do,
K nowing we might die, we shake in panic.

I nterrupting the sound of the wolves, Lucie screamed,
N ow our hearts beat faster, Teigan and I close Sophie's mouth.

T he wolves stopped howling,
H elp signs were put around,
E very one of us was sprinting for our lives.

W e were scared and had nothing to do,
O ther people may not find us,
O thers will get lost too,
D o we have a chance of surviving?
S omeone might find us.

Penelope Carter (11)
Gilbert Inglefield Academy, Leighton Buzzard

My Weird Dreams

M y favourite funny dreams
Y ou see Kermet driving a Lamborghini

W hat is going on? All I see are colours and familiar faces
E ventually, you fall into KFC and Colonel Sanders gives you chicken
I maginary creatures like aliens and griffins squawk and laugh
R idiculous worlds with Lorax and Mike Wazowski
D ing ding, my phone is ringing, it's Shrek

D ucks are quacking all night long
R ocks are falling from the chocolate fountain
E ating tacos and burgers with all the crazy characters
A mong us, all we hear is an alarm
M y imaginary friend started to disappear
S adly the night is over, the day will start, can't wait for the night.

Oscar Adlem (10)
Gilbert Inglefield Academy, Leighton Buzzard

A Holiday I Will Never Forget!

Waves crashing,
Children laughing,
Sips of warm coffee and elders talking,
Jess and I in the cafe, we
re ta;long and gpsso[ng about our day,
We step outside and get a whiff of the warm summer air,
We look at each other and run to the shore,
Collecting seashells to use for decor,
When all of a sudden, ah and the size of a house emerged out of the blue,
And scared a little mouse,
Our eyes widen as the peachy claw grabs the sand,
I take her arm and run away,
Down a valley, around a house,
We look back and we it rise,
Its teeth snapping like mad,
A small child running to his mum,
The authorities came and forced it go to go the deep sea
It calls its home,
We never went back there.

Jasmine Martell (10)
Gilbert Inglefield Academy, Leighton Buzzard

Harrison's Champions League Dream

It happened again, the greatest dream
I found myself back in Spain
Taking the penalty for my team
I felt others in pain

The stadium was full with fans
And my lovely family and nan
They were lifting up their hands
They wish that I really can

All the fans were cheering me to score
Everyone was talking and shouting
But I'm not sure that I'm going to score
I feel like I'm on top of a mountain

I stepped up to shoot
And was going for the kick
Hit hard with my foot
But this moment felt so quick

I closed my eyes in disbelief
Everyone was cheering loudly
I really should've had belief
The next moment, I was lifted in the air highly.

Harrison Reyland (11)
Gilbert Inglefield Academy, Leighton Buzzard

Dreams

I woke with a fright,
As I saw I was surrounded
By drooling monsters,
Some small, some massive,
Some that could kill in a second,
So I started running.
The walls were as blank as paper,
I turned a corner,
And there was a wall,
As I tried to pull myself over,
I felt something grab my foot,
But I wiggled free,
I thought I was there,
There was the door,
I ran, but it was locked
And the big monster walked over.
Suddenly, there were two,
Katana, the taller monster, had the keys,
So I started charging.
Then slashed at his legs.
They came off and then he died.
I got the keys and opened the door,

But then...
I woke up and it was just a dream.

Monty Wisdom (11)
Gilbert Inglefield Academy, Leighton Buzzard

The Detective

The detective in the subway
Waiting for his enemy to strike
Standing like a spike, he is on the train
To work, he isn't a dork.
He gets a case about a murder
Is this a murmur? People taking
The mick while my friend's named
Rick. The detective is making a coffee
As dark as the midnight sky.
It's almost making him cry.
The detective waiting for a response
He is confused and ready
Keep it steady. The detective ready
To strike like a pike, the detective
Ready to catch the murderer, steady
Like a mouse without a douce. Catch!
We caught the killer, it's getting
Dimmer, the detective caught the murderer
It's not a murmur. The detective.

Julian Kildusis (11)
Gilbert Inglefield Academy, Leighton Buzzard

Ice Princess

I 'm dancing in my dance class and take a little break
C lass is over I think as nobody is there, and then the floor shakes
E erie but cool I think as the worlds are not held by chains

P eculiar and strange I'm in ice skates but never was before
R ound the dark corner, there is a white flowery door
I try and open it but to no avail
N ot even a creak it feels like I have lost my boat at sea and my sail
C old and scared I shiver in the midnight sky
E xactly at 1pm I hear a clock and say goodbye
S ee, I don't know why then I hear
S weetie wake up, you're going to be late dear.

Lauren Booth (10)
Gilbert Inglefield Academy, Leighton Buzzard

The Alleyway

I'm running back home,
As fast as I can,
Not looking back to see where I am.
I come across an alleyway,
I don't really care,
I just don't want to know,
What's behind me right there?
The wind is gushing,
The fences are bashing,
There's nothing to do, there's a tornado coming!
I'm panicking, am panicking, jumping up and down,
I know something is lurking around,
I wanna cry, I wanna die.
There's nothing I can do,
Except curl up in a ball,
What's that thing, it smells like a shoe.
I stumble to my feet,
But the next thing I know,
I wake up with a panic...
It was all just a dream.

Keavy Flynn (10)
Gilbert Inglefield Academy, Leighton Buzzard

Space Candy

Once upon a time, in my dreams,
People jumping up and down in ice creams.
Now blood-red Mars,
Was battling with the stars.
I took a step one way,
I really didn't want it to be the end of today.
After a few moments, gummy bears were holding flairs,
Now I was starting to get nightmares.
Suddenly, jelly beans sprinted calmly into the sky,
Honestly, I didn't know beans could fly.
This place was cool - there were no rules,
Fun for all the fools,
Weirdly, the floor below me started to creak,
There was a huge leak!
I fainted and thought I was dead,
But I woke up, my heart racing; I was just happy I was back in bed.

Zac Lee (10)
Gilbert Inglefield Academy, Leighton Buzzard

Abandoned

Smoke and fog combining
from the sky, pouring down
while trees stare at me.

I walk into the wailing woods,
I fall down. Ouch!
I hear howling, owhoo!
From the wolves up to the moon.

And a cow jumping over the moon.
In front of me, what I see,
a haunted house, pitch-black and abandoned.

I tap the door to see if anyone is there.
What I hear is a door creak weirdly.
I see a ghost staring at me.

A witch, spooky and ugly,
putting potions in a bowl.

Cackling as weird,
I wake up my head fastly
looking around, there is nothing,
but me, crouching on my bed.

Mellisa Afram (11)
Gilbert Inglefield Academy, Leighton Buzzard

The Ice Dragon

In the middle of the night
I looked out my window
And saw a dragon, but unlike most, though
This dragon, unlike most, was nice
And this one, unlike most, breathed ice
His skin was as blue as the summer sky
He had scales all over and eyes turquoise and pearly white
His wings were as long as at least a rake
I really, really thought it was fake
But it couldn't have been because he was keeping me awake!
He flew around the neighbourhood for about a mile
And then he looked at me with a joyful smile
And with his breath, in ice, he spelt out 'friend'
And I want to be his friend until the very end.

Daniel McShane (10)
Gilbert Inglefield Academy, Leighton Buzzard

Hogwarts

The broom glistens in the stars,
So bright in the dark grey sky tonight
As I drift through the air,
I bash into a big giant scare
As a dreaded smell fills the air.
Spider sick, brown ick
And Chinese Chomping Cabbage all mashed into one.

Woosh, soosh, a new spell?
Woosh, soosh, a new potion?
Woosh, soosh, food?
Woosh, soosh, I'm going to check it out!

Bottles and jars shaken up to the ceiling
Head to toe colours gleaming
Filled with feathers, eyes and sparkly dust.
This must be the potions room.

The room is filled with stench
As I sit down at the table bench.

Isla Croft (10)
Gilbert Inglefield Academy, Leighton Buzzard

A Dream Void

I closed my eyes,
Trying to avoid more and more lies,
Little did I know I would drift into a void,
Full of wonders and more.

I was suddenly placed in a world where silence was key,
It had endless darkness where stars winked at me,
All alone;
Lost but safe.
It was like a black blanket covering me,
I was weightless,
Calm and free,
Soothing,
Moving across the cosmic sky.

And then, *whoosh!*
I was blown back to reality,
Sleeping soundlessly, silence clouding me,
Back to Earth, safe and cautiously,
Out of my mystical, wonderful dreamland.

Daisy Mowbray (10)
Gilbert Inglefield Academy, Leighton Buzzard

Nightmare

On a bright summer day,
There's nothing like a fresh walk
In the cherry blossom trees.
Boom! Crash!
Lurking in the shadows are your worst nightmares
To take your precious items from your house.
Who will stand up and save the innocent?
Who will be our saviour?
I can't stand around and do nothing,
I have to be the saviour,
To help the innocent,
But I can't do it alone.
So I need to talk to my trustworthy sidekick,
Who is a mastermind,
He knows karate and he's a hacker.
So we locate where they are,
And head into the room of death...

Deon Santo (10)
Gilbert Inglefield Academy, Leighton Buzzard

The Egg

I lie in bed as I wait for something to happen
After about ten minutes, I hear a bang
I walk to my door and see an egg
What's in it, when will it hatch? But most importantly, who put it there?
I pick it up and it is as hot as lava and spotty like a leopard
The next night I hear wings beating hard
I go to see what it is and it is... a dragon
I grab the egg and try to explain
But it won't listen so I give it a chicken nugget
Then she understands
She says a squid stole her egg but she'd burnt the squid to a crisp
The dragon thanks me for returning her egg and flies off.

Samuel Lambert (11)
Gilbert Inglefield Academy, Leighton Buzzard

Dream Valley

I sit up and see the
Sun in the sky
Big and round
In front of me is a hill-like mound
A path swirling round and round
Looks like forever
Then I hear a sound
Birdsong, soft as a spring morning.

I start walking up the patch
Feels like hours
I reach the top
See a strong oak tree
Swaying in the breeze
Hanging from the highest branch
Is a rope swing
I sit down, looking around
I look straight across the valley
And see a sunset
Pink, orange and blue
I drift off back to reality
Hoping to return to Dream Valley soon.

Evie Reynolds (11)
Gilbert Inglefield Academy, Leighton Buzzard

Fire And Ice

Once upon a dream
Fire burning upon my cheeks
I see an ant, small but magical
To transport me to fire and ice
Spinning around through a portal
Why am I here? The ant carries me
I am shocked and amazed - for how can this ant carry me?
We see fire and ice, but nothing beyond
Fog surrounds a cliff edge - I can't see!
The ant slowly falls apart
For it is too hot for the ant. Can't see
Hands in front of me
About to fall off, just one more step.
Off I go, arghh!
Thankfully I wake up safe in bed!

Owen Gould (10)
Gilbert Inglefield Academy, Leighton Buzzard

A Nightmare Of A Haunted Dreamland

A killer is on the loose
That sounds like a goose
I felt eerie
As the police stared at me considering why
I felt spooked
As my friend had to puke
Shivers went down my spine
Until we came across a green lime
Bang!
What was that?
The police disappear
Until we saw something appear
Blood dripped down the wall
Like splash, dark, ketchup down the wall
My friend disappeared too!
But I wasn't afraid of a boo!
I guess I should survive a night
I hope I don't get a fright...

Daisy O'Shea (11)
Gilbert Inglefield Academy, Leighton Buzzard

My Art Career

My dream is to be a successful artist.
In my dream, I make a fortune selling my paintings.
I see people and buildings from where I sit,
On the street, selling paintings.
I may be on my own, but I'm happy with my paintings.
Because of my paintings,
A swarm of people surround me.
It's as loud as an audience at a concert.
It makes me a fortune and I feel good!
And happy!
So I get rich, move in a mansion
And open an art gallery.
If people don't have money,
They get a job to pay it off.

Summer Archer Baker (10)
Gilbert Inglefield Academy, Leighton Buzzard

My Magical Space Dream

Boom! Bang! Crash!
The slow rocket crashed and bashed into the cold, dark moon,
There are eight planets that orbit the chilly sun.
But people and animals live on just one,
In the diamond stars and the beautiful skies,
'Ninety-three percent stardust, with souls made of flames,
We are all just stars who have people's names',
The vector flies provide infinitely scaleable flares,
Which you can simply place over your images, that's it,
No fancy schmancy,
Just immediate.

Aidija Selukaite (11)
Gilbert Inglefield Academy, Leighton Buzzard

Space Station

S pace, you float around forever
P erfectly straight in any direction
A nd you float to the nearest station
C rying on the platform away from
E veryone, no one there to see

S taying silent, the ship arrives
T hen I board, but only an AI
A ppears in front of me
T hen I burst into tears noticing
I can't go home, I'll die in space
O nly on my own, I sit
N ot thinking about life on my own.

Sam Ferguson (11)
Gilbert Inglefield Academy, Leighton Buzzard

Falling

As I slowly drift to sleep,
My eyes can suddenly see the deep,
Pirates tie me up with a loud clank,
And quickly move me to the start of the plank,
They all start talking,
So I obediently start walking,
Plop!
I stop,
The end of the plank has suddenly snapped off,
I gulp and look back,
But the world has turned black,
I start falling and falling,
I'm crying and calling,
I wake up out of breath,
I felt so close to death,
Thank goodness I'm in bed.

Casey Reed
Gilbert Inglefield Academy, Leighton Buzzard

The Upside Down

The Upside Down is an opposite world,
It has monsters and insects galore.
It is never nice; it always has mice,
And no one ever asks questions.

And if anyone asks questions,
Someone always knows why.
But still, just make sure you don't,
Never pet the goat,
And you will do just fine.

The monsters are evil and cruel,
They always are funny,
And very, very clumsy.
But if you annoy them, they will be boring,
And they will just not be the same.

Alice Robertson-Hills (11)
Gilbert Inglefield Academy, Leighton Buzzard

My Important Dream About Arsenal

A rsenal kick off and fans are crazy as the atmosphere is brilliant!
R umbling stomach at half-time as butterflies join my stomach.
S eparate fans mouthing each other in the alley stand.
E mirates Stadium is going wild as there is a winner!
N ext, I go into the Arsenal dressing room after a 3-1 win.
A t last, I met Arsenal's star, Declan Rice, who scored the 90+8 winner!
L ater, my dad and I got pizza. What a day!

Lewis Payne (11)
Gilbert Inglefield Academy, Leighton Buzzard

Nightmares

N ights where dreams turn bad
I n total fear, I stepped forward
G oing forward, I heard something in the bush
H orrified, I ran away while hearing something
T he forest went on forever, I turned around
M y heart stopped, it disappeared behind the trees
A slight sound made me jump
R ight behind stood a monster
E ventually, he grabbed me
S uddenly, I woke up safe in my bed.

Mason Hollingsworth (11)
Gilbert Inglefield Academy, Leighton Buzzard

My First-Ever Fortnite Crown Win

We went to kill boss Nisha
But someone comes from behind, we kill Chirbi
In fencing fields
We have a riot shield
We kill Nisha
But ninja steals my Mythic
We later go on to get thirty kills
I see a crown and I pick it up
A lion has a massive roar
Wait lions in Fortnite
Peterbot pushes me into Storm
He's flying, he has hacks
But I still headshot snipe him 303
I shot 200!
We win the FNCS Finals!

Max Bellamy (10)
Gilbert Inglefield Academy, Leighton Buzzard

Where Am I?

W hat is going on? The only thing in sight is an endless void.
H ow did I get here?
E veryone is missing, where did they go?
R eal? Fake? I don't have a clue.
E scape? Should I try to escape?

A m I dreaming?
M orning, when will it come?

I have finally woken up and it was only a dream, but a strange one like no other I've ever had before.

Maggie Grimes (11)
Gilbert Inglefield Academy, Leighton Buzzard

Kangaroos

K angaroos are bouncy marsupials
A live in Australia, that's their home
N eeding shade when they're warm.
G etting water from a storm
A ll kangaroos are happy and free.
R eal joeys live in the pouch.
O nly when they're babies until they're
O lder, soon they will be like their mum
S earching for their fun-filled feast!

April Lemon (11)
Gilbert Inglefield Academy, Leighton Buzzard

The Game

Players walk through the tunnel
very slowly they step onto the pitch.
Everyone cheers Thomas! Thomas! Thomas!
Suddenly they all disappear
and all I'm left with is I.
Was this a dream?
All I hear is *thump, thump, thump*
and then I finally realise it's my mum walking up the flight of stairs
and at that moment I knew
it was a dream.

Thomas Millett (11)
Gilbert Inglefield Academy, Leighton Buzzard

Football

F un football is the best dream ever.
O fficially, you don't have to be clever!
O h my god, I scored the winning goal!
T he mascot said, "You're on a roll!"
B ang! The ball went zooming into my face.
A ll of a sudden, I started to pace.
L uckily, it wasn't too bad.
L ast of all, my parents are extremely mad!

Nicole Botez (10)
Gilbert Inglefield Academy, Leighton Buzzard

Alien Bunny

The alien bunny looks very funny,
The alien bunny was once called Bubby.
It makes weird noises like *bibbly bubbly*,
It lives in this place called outer space Dreamland.
It loves to eat blobby plants.
They make him do hilarious farts.
He has this thing where he has a lot of bling.
He shows it off to his fellow chimps
And he also likes to eat spaghetti beats.

Theo Rye (11)
Gilbert Inglefield Academy, Leighton Buzzard

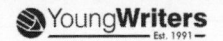

Have You Seen The Girl On The Moon?

Have you seen the girl on the moon?

Or have you seen her somewhere else?
Will I see her anytime soon?

At the peak of darkness
You can hear her tune
And dancing with kindness

The diamond dress flowing around like a waterfall
Her hair was shining as bright as a star
It was like she got the dress from the mall

It was a perfect dream.

Hannah Booth (10)
Gilbert Inglefield Academy, Leighton Buzzard

The Dreamer

Last night, there was a blurry blob
Bouncing off the walls
While reading the entire English dictionary.

Last night, there were some space giraffes
Hurdling over spaceships
While swinging their necks around.

Last night, I dreamt of chinchillas
With laser eyes and lightsabers.

Last night, there were chilli cheese bites
Dancing around.

Tommy Ogden (10)
Gilbert Inglefield Academy, Leighton Buzzard

Car Journey

C an I escape?
A m I stuck here?
R eality has run away!

J ust can't stay!
O h, I see a scary lagoon
U pwards is a shimmering moon
R eady to go home
N ow all I can do is dream about home
E ven though I'm sad, looking up I see a star
Y es, all a dream in the car.

Rose Whatman (10)
Gilbert Inglefield Academy, Leighton Buzzard

Spiders

S uddenly I awake in a huge endless cave
P ools of blood dripping from webs
I look around to see no human in sight
D eep within the cave, a spider queen lies
E ntering the darkness, I fall and I lie
R uthless spiders scramble around
S creaming scaredly, I awake in my soft, snuggly bed.

Cody Francis (10)
Gilbert Inglefield Academy, Leighton Buzzard

Conflict

I'm in a war town, no peace at all,
With dissembled houses and only one wall,
Bombs on the ground, no way out,
All alone with some doubt,
Guns neatly scattered about,
A town with no water, a town with a draught,
People who were hiding didn't make it out,
The town used to be happy,
Then the lights dimmed down.

Tiana Chase (11)
Gilbert Inglefield Academy, Leighton Buzzard

Peppa Pig, The Serial Killer

High in the sky between two mountains,
A million feet above the clouds,
I'm on a tightrope with no safety,
So if I fall, I will die,
Then I hear a noise behind me,
It's a giant Peppa Pig serial killer,
With a dagger in her hand,
Running towards me... I fall to the land.
Did I die?

Jake Bromley (10)
Gilbert Inglefield Academy, Leighton Buzzard

Nowhere

N othing there, wow, absolutely nothing.
O ut of nowhere, I heard shuffling.
W hat if this is a dream?
H ow do I get out of here? What if I die?
E very cloud was grey, gloomy and dismal.
R oaring at me, I started to run.
E ven though I had nowhere to go.

Isabella Higgins (11)
Gilbert Inglefield Academy, Leighton Buzzard

Ava-Rose's Dream

In my dream one night,
I suddenly rise in the sky,
Above my town floating in the clouds,
Running in the air suspended in mid-air,
Scared as I fly so very high, I can almost touch the sky,
I realise I have the freedom to soar,
Flying is fun until you hit the floor... *Crash!*

Ava-Rose Barry (11)
Gilbert Inglefield Academy, Leighton Buzzard

Dreams

D iving through cotton candy
R ivers, to flying over Mars, to
E nding the world from nightmares to dreams.
A world beyond time till
M um wakes you up. Just
S o it was just part of your imagination.

Jamie Fletcher (11)
Gilbert Inglefield Academy, Leighton Buzzard

Abandoned

In my dreams most nights,
There are flickering lights.
Balloons floating,
Crows croaking,
Factory crumbling down,
Skeletons with big frowns.
Trees bending,
Text messages sending.

Ronnie Millson (11)
Gilbert Inglefield Academy, Leighton Buzzard

My Dream Was The Worst Ever

I saw my friend going whiter from blood loss,
And I could smell my friend's rotting body.
Why was I vomiting?
But I was okay.
Why did I hear screaming?
Why was I going deaf?

Xavier Procter (11)
Gilbert Inglefield Academy, Leighton Buzzard

While You Are Sleeping

N obody likes it
I t's as mean as can be
G o in your closet and you will be scared
H orrifying dreams
T errifying dreams
M eet you in my dreams
A nother nightmare will come
R occo has come to the end - dead
E xplain how you make nightmares

D reams
R elease your lovely dreams
E ven if the nightmare scares you, let it go.
A mazing
M emories will never leave you
S weet dreams.

Seth Wright (10)
Heyford Park School, Upper Heyford

Haunting You At Night

In the night, they come
But only some.
Wherever they are from
They are scum!

They perch on your windowsill
Ready to kill
Unless you are ill
Then they have no will.
Don't offer them a seat
As they will eat your fleshy meat.
In whatever biome
They will roam.

They come at dark
Running wild in the park.
When the light is switched off
They are friends with the moth.
In the torchlight
They hide as they might.

They would battle the good
If they could.
When they're in the right mood
They call each other dude.

They will create blood
When they are misjudged.
So just pinch yourself
To keep your health.

They'll haunt you at night
Away from the light.
A monster is a nightmare's best friend
But their relationships never mend.

As you wake, you hear a scream
So be prepared to face the bad dream
And say goodnight
To the beastly sight.

Willow Steele (10)
Heyford Park School, Upper Heyford

Dream World

Once I had a dream
A dream about a dream world
A world where everything's a dream
And everything comes true.

And once I fell asleep
And woke up in a dream world
Where everything was pink
And I was all alone.

I felt so calm and happy
That I was in a dream world
There was gentle music playing
Because I was in a dream world.

But then I realised
That it was just a dream
A dream about a dream world
Where I was all alone.

Dasha Bochkala (10)
Heyford Park School, Upper Heyford

Flower

Tulips and daffodils,
Mine is a rose,
As red as a ruby,
No one else knows.

As I sleep, it blooms once again.

It's at the heart of the village,
Nice as can be,
As you look round the corner,
Then you will see.

As I sleep, it blooms once again.

After school, I only see light,
When I come home, nothing is right,
As I run around the corner, I see it there,
Everything apart from my rose is bare.

Charlotte Waton (9)
Heyford Park School, Upper Heyford

Animals

There were once two kids,
They were animal lovers.
They were relaxing until a baby lion came and cried.
The girls didn't know what to do.
They saw the mummy lion shouting for help in a net.
The bad man did it and his name was Bob.

The girls used their powers to stop Bob.
The net broke and the mummy was free.
She attacked the bad man.
He started to run away.
"Yes!" cried the girls. "We did it!"

Ivana Simakoski (9)
Heyford Park School, Upper Heyford

The Amazing Space

Flying like a free man,
Throughout the outer space,
Touching the stars,
This is what I dream about.

Hovering over great large gassy planets,
And minuscule watery planets,
Touching the pillow clouds,
This is what I dream about.

Going through the Milky Way,
Adventuring around the hundred billion galaxies,
Darting through worlds upon worlds,
This is what I dream about.

Lucas Bird (9)
Heyford Park School, Upper Heyford

Dreams Gone Wrong

N o more great dreams for you,
I gnore the tall monsters under your bed,
G et the talking teddy to sleep,
H ate the world of dreams,
T he bed is haunted with nightmares,
M ake something to calm you down,
A s you dream they come,
R ace the bad,
E verything disappearing around you,
S ave yourself.

Dylan Pugh (9)
Heyford Park School, Upper Heyford

Sweet World (A Dream)

When I go to Sweet World...

I meet Candy Man
He has gumdrop eyes and a liquorice mouth
I really am his biggest fan
We jump on gummy trampolines and run about
We lick the lollipop trees
We lie on the icing grass
We try to catch sugar flake leaves floating on the breeze
Oh it really does go so fast.

Juniper Zeyfert (10)
Heyford Park School, Upper Heyford

Dream Of A Garden

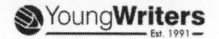

Dream of a garden,
A garden with flowers,
A garden with powers.

You can see a tree,
This tree has dreams,
This tree has nightmares,
This tree has cares.

You can see a girl,
This girl has a necklace of pearls,
Her hair is long and luscious,
Her dress has bright, majestic flowers.

Georgia Bichard (10)
Heyford Park School, Upper Heyford

Silly Barret

Dogs all around the beautiful land,
Nothing in Dog Land is blank.

I go there every time I sleep,
Nothing there is bleak.

Candy the cat is my pet,
The best buddy I ever met!

Soon a rabbit stole our carrots,
But we forgave him 'cause he's Barret.

Lea Smit (9)
Heyford Park School, Upper Heyford

My Dream

D anger lurks around every corner,
R unning, walking, driving, hoarding,
E very noise has a risk,
A roaring engine noise ahead,
M aybe friend, maybe foe,
S o, I'm not sticking around to find out, bye!

Jack Laker (10)
Heyford Park School, Upper Heyford

Dreams

D reams of imagination,
R ainbows in the clouds,
E ndless happiness,
A nd don't boast out loud,
M agic is alive,
S ome of us have nightmares, but all of us have dreams.

Jessica Luciano (9)
Heyford Park School, Upper Heyford

Magical Forest In My Dreams

It was just a forest
Until these gorillas came along
It turned into volcanoes
And city mines
People running around like spiders.

Rhys Viglieno (10)
Heyford Park School, Upper Heyford

All The Things I Dream About

D ogs
R obins
E ating chicken nuggets
A pples
M altese poodles
S weets.

Jane Keenan (10)
Heyford Park School, Upper Heyford

My Gymnast Dream

It was a subtle night, all was silent
I was standing there, nothing was violent.
The competition was about to start
I felt a sharp pain in my heart.

Maybe it was something I had for lunch.
Or maybe it was something I had for brunch.
It was vault first, I was with my coach
Now it was time for me to approach.

I got my highest score on vault!
It was my best-ever somersault!
Next was bars, they looked very large!
One of the opponents started to barge!

Next up it was time for floor
Which is certainly not a bore!
Now it was time for beam
I wonder what theme?

Suddenly there was a pain!
I hope it's not a sprain.
Here are the results, I wonder what they'll be?
Announced is the winner, oh yes it's me!

Sadie Muir (9)
Kirkpatrick Fleming Primary School, Lockerbie

The Magic Dream

I woke up this morning as fit as can be
To have breakfast with family
I went to school as happy as can be
But something was off with me
At lunchtime me and my friend were having lunch
I was eating beans, she was making a crunch
There was a thud as loud as can be
Unicorns came crashing not me
One went to my friend and one came to me
And it stole my beans, I was mad as can be
But not as mad as my friend when it stole her cheese
She ran and charged and shouted, "Freeze!"
My friend jumped at it and we got our food
Now we were in a very good mood
That was when I woke up with a smile like a beam
I told everyone and now I call it the magic dream!

Lilly Woodward (9)
Kirkpatrick Fleming Primary School, Lockerbie

Roller Coasters

R oller coasters, roller coasters, they're so much fun!
O n the carousel where lots of kids laugh.
L ovely sweets and treats.
L ots of shrieks and screams.
E verybody's having fun, especially me!
R iding roller coasters is my favourite thing to do.

C otton candy to nibble on.
O h, such a dream!
A ll of us are going on the big bumpy one.
S tars are beginning to shine in the sky.
T he day is nearly over.
E verybody is starting to get sleepy now.
R oller coasters are just about to stop.
S leepy now, I can't wait to have a dream.

Clara Little (9)
Kirkpatrick Fleming Primary School, Lockerbie

Candyland

In my dream every night,
Sweets and clouds appear in my sight
Every night I am on cloud nine high above the sky
Here comes Willy Wonka with a nice grin as a surprise
He has a house made out of gingerbread
With chocolate bars, which are fun.
With nice blue eyes, he looks at me with a twinkle like the sun
We have come to this place to be friends
Glancing left and right.
All I see is chocolate swirling,
I close my eyes, dreading to still be there
I open them, I fear crying if I dare!
I wake up to be safe and sound
In my bed where I can be found.

Sophia Shields (9)
Kirkpatrick Fleming Primary School, Lockerbie

The Candy Land

T he monsters and clowns were chasing me.
"**H** elp!" The monsters and clowns took me.
E ven a scary wizard came to the dungeon.

"**C** ome and save me!" I shouted.
A lthough the wizard was with the clowns.
"**N** o! Save me!" I shouted,
"**D** on't go to them! Save me!"
Y et I still tried to shout, "Help me!"

"**L** et me out!" I shouted
A nd somebody came to save me.
N ow, I wake up in bed,
D reams can be scary.

Elsie McCracken (9)
Kirkpatrick Fleming Primary School, Lockerbie

Hot Chocolate Land

C hocolate is my favourite.
H ot chocolate is warm and tasty, but the normal hot chocolate flavour is the best.
O thers say chocolate is better than hot chocolate, but I don't agree.
C hocolate cookie dipped in hot chocolate is so good!
O reos are my favourite cookies. What are yours?
L uxury liquid, a lovely, luxurious drink.
A nyone can have a hot chocolate.
T here are other hot chocolate flavours.
E veryone loves dreaming about hot chocolate!

Vilte Narbutaite (8)
Kirkpatrick Fleming Primary School, Lockerbie

Mars Adventure

A fter my spaceship crashed on Mars
L ovely planets surround me
I cky aliens everywhere, they make me want to scream
E verywhere I look I see beautiful twinkling stars
N ooks and crannies everywhere, let's go explore

D eep down on Mars, now I hear weird sounds
R umbling and creaking... But I see a light
E scaping might be hard
A fter all, the ground surface is as hot as coal
M ars has been great, but I need to get back home!

Finlay Wylie (9)
Kirkpatrick Fleming Primary School, Lockerbie

Chocolate Land

C amping is where me and Mum go.
H owever, there was a fire, so we had to go home.
O ur house was covered with chocolate.
C hocolate was on the walls and the tables.
O ur table had chocolate bars and eggs.
L ately, it was getting dark.
A wizard came into our house.
T oday, he said, "Open a chocolate bar!" It had a golden ticket.
E arly now, it was just a dream.

Lily Rae (9)
Kirkpatrick Fleming Primary School, Lockerbie

Just Desserts

D on't go in, you will lose yourself,
E nchanted things can be in there,
S cared, what will you do? Nothing there to save you.
S piders, no, but what's that, a clown?
E verything you have, you run and run,
R unning, then you suddenly wake up.
T he clown is no longer there, it's just a dream.

Eddie Woodward (9)
Kirkpatrick Fleming Primary School, Lockerbie

Nightmare

N ightmare
I was with my friend Vilte
G ot to get out of here
H orrifying clown
T he clown had terrifying eyes
M ade a scream at the top of our voice
A re you scared?
R unning back home now
E scaped my nightmare!

Eidigh Davidson (8)
Kirkpatrick Fleming Primary School, Lockerbie

Paris

Oh no, where am I?
This is one funny dream for me.
Wait, where are my mum and dad?
Is that the Eiffel Tower I see?
I can't believe it, I'm in Paris
But no one is around, how can that be?
I wake up all snuggly in bed.
I just can't get Paris out of my head!

Jack Balmer (9)
Kirkpatrick Fleming Primary School, Lockerbie

Dream

D ream, it's weird, you can't get out unless someone wakes you,
R obots could take you away, you could never see the light of day ever again,
E verything could go wrong or right.
A nything could happen.
M y oh my, I don't know what to do!

Cooper Richardson (8)
Kirkpatrick Fleming Primary School, Lockerbie

Dreamland

D reamland starts with candy and cake.
R esisting is hard for most, but I am one of them.
E ating is all I want, but it is hard to eat all in one.
A s I walk forward I find a yummy, gooey gingerbread house.
M y dream had come true.

Isabella Thomson (8)
Kirkpatrick Fleming Primary School, Lockerbie

Dream

D reaming about exploring the cave,
R unning with my friend.
E ventually, we find the extremely fierce lion,
A rghh, we are all very scared,
M aking a run for it super fast. At last, I wake, it was only a dream.

Wills Halliday (9)
Kirkpatrick Fleming Primary School, Lockerbie

Dreaming About Chocolate Pie

D ays were past, I made chocolate pie.
R oasting chocolate pie in my hands.
"**E** at up!" said Nanny.
"**A** nd by the way, Nanny, you are the best!"
M ost of the pie was cool, the rest was hot!

Joseph Graham (9)
Kirkpatrick Fleming Primary School, Lockerbie

Animals Are The Best!

A nimals are cute
N esting in their beds
I n the morning, they're hopping, hopping
M agical creatures, we need to protect
A nimals make me happy
L ove animals, what a perfect dream!

Alice Ewings (8)
Kirkpatrick Fleming Primary School, Lockerbie

Dream

D reaming about driving a Scania V8 wagon 770.
R iding to Edinburgh.
E nd of the journey.
A ccidents happen! The wagon tipped over.
M y trailer was overloaded.
S cared was how I felt.

Jack Haillday (9)
Kirkpatrick Fleming Primary School, Lockerbie

Dream

D reaming about a hot summer holiday,
R eally excited to go to Spain,
E xcited to see the palm trees and ocean,
A t the pool is where I love to swim,
M aking memories with my parents.

Louie Johnston (9)
Kirkpatrick Fleming Primary School, Lockerbie

Dreaming

D reaming about a magical horse
R iding the horses with my friends
E vening time begins
A nd it all changes
M y friends are gone
S ave them from angry dragons!

Jasmine Murray (9)
Kirkpatrick Fleming Primary School, Lockerbie

Dream

D reaming in the jungle, I am not scared.
R egretting not being scared,
E verything went quiet.
A nd a tiger came out of nowhere. Arghh!
M um, thank you for saving me!

Sam Rae (8)
Kirkpatrick Fleming Primary School, Lockerbie

The Dream Void

D reaming in the dream void
R eality no longer exists
E xtraterrestrials are here
A m I safe, what will happen?
M an, it was only a dream!

Soren Corkill (8)
Kirkpatrick Fleming Primary School, Lockerbie

Dream

D reaming about spiders,
R eally happy, I love spiders.
E xcited because they climb up my leg,
A ll in my shed,
M y dad is with me!

Harley-J Ayres (8)
Kirkpatrick Fleming Primary School, Lockerbie

Once Upon A Candy World

Once upon a candy world,
A world of cake houses, lolly trees,
Cotton candy clouds and people who were
Very crazy
They run around the place,
But the most crazy thing is
They are made of gumdrops,
M&M's and Skittles,
A magical waterfall that is,
A nice, calming colour,
Magical animals,
Once upon a candy world.

I walk around for a long time and
Find a solid chocolate cave,
I go in it and find a clean,
Shining diamond,
I try to touch it but
The people, or should I say
Candy,

Pull me out and
Shut the cave,
Solid shut.
Once upon a candy world.

I go back to the cave and see
Guards standing there,
So I leave and never go back.
I go to see the candy
People to ask them why
I can't go in the cave.
I get there and they say
It's dangerous,

So I believe them
And never go back.
Once upon a candy world.

Kara Corkill (9)
Our Lady Of Lourdes RC Primary School, Bolton

The Land Of Powers

A land of magical creatures,
They look like gigantic green monsters,
The others are like little yellow aliens,
The terrifying creatures eat,
Weird red fruit in it.

Witches plotting magic things,
In cauldrons and a sturdy glamorous wall,
So nobody can get past it,
And nobody will steal the magical flower.

When it was night, green little eyes,
Pop when it's midnight and eat caterpillars,
Because they are hungry
And they didn't eat anything in the day.

At midnight, angry wolves go out in the dark,
So villagers go inside,
Scared that they'll eat everyone in the village,
But the wolves only eat leaves and mice.

The trees of the village hear the skies,
And know it's time to report to the stars,
So the stars then go outside,
And then it turns into night.

Antoni Joseph (8)
Our Lady Of Lourdes RC Primary School, Bolton

Once Upon A Dream

A land of magical, enchanted creatures,
Rivers as clear as crystal balls,
Cherry blossom trees reach for the sky,
The sun shines as bright as heaven,
Once upon a dream.

As the sky turns to night,
The sky turns into a twilight blanket,
The cascading waterfall takes my breath as it never stops,
Stars were as bright as sparkling sapphires,
The whispers of fairies' wings in my ear,
Once upon a dream.

On top of the clouds, there is,
A castle for fairies,
Cherry rose flowers flow down,
The mountain like blood,
Trees are spies reporting back to the stars,
Roaring little goblins try to scare me,
Whoosh! The clouds pass me,
In my dreamland in my
Nella fantasia.

Darlene Acheampong (9)
Our Lady Of Lourdes RC Primary School, Bolton

Nella Fantasia

A land of verdant forests and
mountains everywhere you go
Cherry-red roses are blood dripping
Down the mountain,
Breathtaking, enchanted, verdant
Castles hiding behind the crystal
waterfall
Nella Fantasia.

Microscopic mysterious little cottages
Crumbling at the second when the door opens,
Blue waterfalls as clear as a crystal
Covering the planet like a huge, fluffy
blanket.
Nella Fantasia.

Pink, cute roses and tulips smelling
So delightful anywhere I go
Crystal-clear blue lightning protecting
The planet from scavengers,
Vines rubbing on my
Glimmering body taking me
To his castle.
Nella Fantasia.

Isla Barnes (9)
Our Lady Of Lourdes RC Primary School, Bolton

Doughnuts Land

A land of mystery doughnuts
And yummy sprinkly houses made from a mixture of doughnut dough,
The roof dripping with custard like a flaming rocket,
Over an icing hill, there is a bridge ready to lead you through Doughnut Forest,
The bridge is made of lots of special things like golden fizzing doughnut cream,
Once upon a dream.

The sky sizzles down like a mountain,
Little droplets of jam cream,
Old stepmoms live in the joyful cottage,
The Doughnut Forest has lots of doughnut plants and doughnut monsters.
Once upon a dream.

And you can smell doughnut cream,
And from the sky, you can hear sprinkles shiver to the ground,
Once upon a dream.

Daniel Shennowo (8)
Our Lady Of Lourdes RC Primary School, Bolton

Once Upon A Dream

A land of candyfloss, lollipops and doughnuts,
I glanced behind me and lots of sticky, bright lollipops burst angrily and sobbed,
The sweet, pink candyfloss shone as the clouds in the turquoise sky,
Once upon a dream.

The ice cream was like caramel dripping everywhere,
The huge white chocolate cookies
Shine as bright as the sun,
Once upon a dream.

Doughnuts battled each other so one can be on the throne,
Sprinkles fall down like rain onto candy houses,
The cascading waterfall takes my breath away as it is made from white chocolate,
As it turns to night the sky turns into a twilight blanket in the sky
Once upon a dream.

Ruby Smalley (8)
Our Lady Of Lourdes RC Primary School, Bolton

Once Upon A Dream

The clouds were glimmering like a shiny glitter bomb,
Chocolate dripping down through the chocolate fountain,
Gingerbread men both chattering together and enjoying their day,
Candyfloss soft like fluffy marshmallows,
Once upon a dream.

Lollipops were laughing and enjoying their game and playing together,
Caramel dripping down from the clouds as it's raining,
Rocks were laughing and being friends and enjoying,
Once upon a dream.

Trees smell like strawberries, houses made out of ginger,
With a toffee door, rainbow sprinkles, and tiny bits of chocolate,
The ground shaking like crystal just cracked,
Once upon a dream.

Amina Khan (8)
Our Lady Of Lourdes RC Primary School, Bolton

Nella Fantasia

Nella Fantasia
A world of any food you could imagine.
A chocolate waterfall, lollipop trees, and even gingerbread houses.
You can hear little noises of gingerbread people.

Nella Fantasia
Chocolate rivers flow through the sweety forest.
Everything you can see, you can eat!
You can see giant chocolate bars and sweets
And even giant candyfloss.

Nella Fantasia
Clouds are candyfloss, rain is sprinkles.
The floor is brownies, the mud is fudge cake,
And the rocks are marshmallows.
And even the animals are chocolate,
Even clothes are maple syrup!

Nella Fantasia.

Jack Porter (8)
Our Lady Of Lourdes RC Primary School, Bolton

My Fantasy World

When I woke up
I found myself in this cool but calm place
It was full of dreams and wishes
I'm so glad that I visited my dream world
Because it is fun.

Once upon a dream.

Time had passed and I was getting bored
Until hot-air ballons shot up into the twilight sky
In my tree house/cabin
I heard loud drops falling from the sky
Only to find out it was raining rainbow sprinkles.

Once upon a dream.

I was so excited for what tomorrow would bring
But for now
I'm going to dream of more adventures like this one.

Once upon a dream.

Poppy Nesbitt (8)
Our Lady Of Lourdes RC Primary School, Bolton

Once Upon A Dream

Once upon a dream,
A land of magical people teleported to an unknown ginormous forest,
Once upon a dream,
Small fairies whispering in a secret language,
Their voices were as quiet as a mouse,
Tip-toeing through the amazing deep forest,
Once upon a dream,
Tall trees swaying in the wind,
Trees as tall as mountains,
Dancing to the sound of the howling wind,
Once upon a dream,
The sweet magical smell tickling my nose,
The little red doors were flapping in the wind like paper,
Little eyes peeping through the tiny windows, birds tweeting,
Once upon a dream.

George Taylor (9)
Our Lady Of Lourdes RC Primary School, Bolton

Once Upon A Dream

A land of living astronauts inside the moon,
Spaceships zooming down back to Earth,
The sound of complete nothingness around me and everyone else
Listening to the spaceships say their last goodbyes,
Up, up in my dreams.

Astronauts sat in houses packing the last things,
Glimmering balls of light known as stars twinkling in the night sky,
One after another taking off to different planets,
Up, up in my dreams.

Skyscrapers as tall as the universe,
Stars brighter than the sun,
Crystal-like stars disappearing and reappearing,
Up, up in my dreams.

Holly Carberry (9)
Our Lady Of Lourdes RC Primary School, Bolton

Once Upon A Dream

A land of magical surprises, magical animals.

A magical ocean as clear as diamonds,
Flying puppies barking as you approach them,
The magic ocean whooshing into my ear,
Once upon a dream.

The dogs barking as loud as a trumpet,
The flying dogs are as cuddly as a teddy,
The whispers of the dogs' fluffy ears when they flop,
Once upon a dream,

The never-ending chocolate tempting me to eat it,
The magical snow globe that can make it snow whenever you want,
The kind shopkeeper welcoming you to his shop,
Once upon a dream.

Molly Newns (9)
Our Lady Of Lourdes RC Primary School, Bolton

Once Upon A Fantasy World

A world of gargantuan,
Enchanted library and cloud village,
Books as interesting as history.
Tree clouds swish,
Side to side,
Once upon a fantasy world.

Library is as quiet as a mouse,
Spellbooks are fascinating.
Once you open them
You will build a wall of knowledge.
Also smelling the sweet,
Cotton candy smell,
Once upon a fantasy world.

The waterfall drips day and night,
A wand made for making the waterfall
Even magical.
The river is as shiny and interesting as diamonds,
Once upon a fantasy world.

Leander Sakala (8)
Our Lady Of Lourdes RC Primary School, Bolton

Once Upon A Dream

Once upon a dream,
A land full of sweets and cake,
The towers as tall as a pencil.
Velvet cake planes up above the candyfloss.
Once upon a dream.

Once upon a dream,
The houses with caramel cake, inside of the house,
The cars with cream at the side of each door.
It was never raining or night, it was always morning.
Once upon a dream.

Once upon a dream,
The houses were as big as an elephant,
The rocks were made out of carrot cake,
The waves swoosh in front of the houses,
Once upon a dream.

Gabriel Cullis (8)
Our Lady Of Lourdes RC Primary School, Bolton

Once Upon A Dream

In a land of legends and paradise,
A magical fairy tree of wishes and dreams,
Goblins and fairies,
Fizzing with excitement and magic.

Glazed icing of fairy treats fizzing in my mouth,
My feet floating down the stairs built from dreams and wishes,
The sound of chattering and giggling from fairy parties,
Magic oozing from every room of this magical castle.

The sunset glows and the light seeps,
Under the windows and doors,
Bringing the magical morning inside,
As fairy voices quiet and slide into dreams.

Lorenza Grae Lopez (8)
Our Lady Of Lourdes RC Primary School, Bolton

Nella Fantasia

In Treetopia it is peaceful,
The only sound you hear is leaves crunching like crisps when you step on them,
As well as water dripping from leaves,
Leaves whooshing in the air and landing on mystical creature's heads.

Trees as tall as a skyscraper, they are going to touch the moon,
An endless pit of doom,
Goblins murmuring in goblin language,
Brutes bending iron,
A floating castle and flying monkeys,
Goblins' houses made out of trees,
Sometimes battles go on in the distance.

Grayson Booker-Bryon (8)
Our Lady Of Lourdes RC Primary School, Bolton

Once Upon A Dream

The sound of brilliant birds chirping in the deep forest,
Tiny leaves swishing and swooshing about next to trees,
Trees rush in the deep dark forest.
Once upon a dream

The rain silently dripped from the damp tree,
The smell of your nana's freshly made cookies at home,
Trees whispering to one another,
The deep, spacious forest whispered.
Once upon a dream

The tree boomed in the dark forest,
The little goblins jog in the deep, dark forest, lonely.
Once upon a dream.

Ollie Haslam (9)
Our Lady Of Lourdes RC Primary School, Bolton

A Magic World

In my magic world,
A castle up on a mountain with lots of villagers inside,
A magical celebration of laughter and magic,
The windows of the castle light and bright.

In my magic world,
Fairies and pixies dance and prance,
Rooms full of treasure and jewels,
Diamonds hanging from every doorway.

In my magic world,
Music tinkling from faraway ballrooms,
Light glowing and twinkling,
Fairies flutter excitedly from room to room.

Elliott Leach (8)
Our Lady Of Lourdes RC Primary School, Bolton

Nella Fantasia

A land of chattering pizzas,
Then, houses danced and sang as we passed them,
Pizzas and pizzas note in my ear,
Nella Fantasia.

Trees the shape of your pizza dreams,
Clouds full of the sparkling crust,
The sky is a soft blanket of pepperoni,
Nella Fantasia.

Pizzas sang and danced as we walked on,
The secret pizza powers are still unknown,
Nella Fantasia.

Jacob Smally (8)
Our Lady Of Lourdes RC Primary School, Bolton

Nella Fantasia

A land of mythical, magical creatures,
Fairies and goblins chattering and scampering around my wrists,
Laughter coming from mossy trees,
Whispering goblins telling secrets only they know,
Nella Fantasia.

Witches stand around boiling cauldrons,
Stars sparkle as bright as sapphires,
The twilight sky as blue as the deep blue sea,
Nella Fantasia.

Clara O'Brien (9)
Our Lady Of Lourdes RC Primary School, Bolton

Upon A Dream

This land is loving and kind,
Believe the candy people,
It's alive!
Once upon a dream.

Talking butterflies, *whoosh!*
And people hop happily,
Once upon a dream.

Rosalie Parkinson (9)
Our Lady Of Lourdes RC Primary School, Bolton

Once Upon A Dream

Once upon a dream
A land full of machinery and mystical creatures
Some were building
Some were playing
Some were mining for resources
Once upon a dream.

Aham Zubair (8)
Our Lady Of Lourdes RC Primary School, Bolton

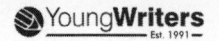

Once Upon A Dream

In my gigantic science factory world
There are sea creatures and
Caves full of goblins and terrifying monsters
Once upon a dream
Carts crashing and whooshing.

Archie Earp (8)
Our Lady Of Lourdes RC Primary School, Bolton

The Clouds Dream

On a starry night, I went to bed with a dream in my head,
Boom - what should I do?
I'm now on what felt like a candyfloss cloud,
There are clouds of wonder,
Clouds of shame,
Clouds to never be seen again,
The next moment, I realise I'm on a cloud going into space,
Space - wow!
I'm on the Milky Way,
Just like the one in the amazing chocolate place,
Oh no, I've just realised I'm on a cloud shaped like a gnome,
Floating to who knows where,
I sing my poem, then fall into a black hole of sleep,
Waking up realising it was all a dream,
Then I had a feeling of shame thinking how I thought my space and cloud dream were true,
But how could I be so foolish?
Absolutely foolish,
I was still in a space mood in my space bedroom,
Thinking maybe it is true up there,

Who knows? There might be a cloud space bedroom,
Clouds are humans, too.

Ava Tooes (10)
St Peter's Catholic Primary School, Waterlooville

My Dreams Are Amazing

M y dreams are a wonderful thing,
Y ou can even see,

D id you know it's as lovely as a flower?
R eally, it's amazing sugar houses, honey flowers, dancers everywhere,
E verything you could imagine,
A ll you could love,
M y dreams are amazing; come and see,
S mall shrimp and massive monkeys,

A ll you could love, all you could see,
R apid speed, lightning fast,
E xtraordinary small elephants,

A nyone like cake?
M y dreams have cake the size of Jupiter,
A ll things to love,
Z ip zap, rainbows everywhere,
I magine a life like this,
N o one would want more,
G ood things in this land. Uh, uh - no bad stuff allowed.

Isla Jordan (9)
St Peter's Catholic Primary School, Waterlooville

Amber

Amber is a lovely little girl, as sweet as a flower. She will dance all day in the sun or rain so here are some things about her.

- **A** mazing at dancing, oh yes she is. She dances in the rain and sploshes in the puddles.
- **M** agnificent at reading. She's reading a book per day like Matilda the bookworm in that movie, do you know it?
- **B** est at sewing. She creates purple, spotty dresses and pink ballerina tutus. When she wore her dress, it smiled at her.
- **E** ggcellent at reading. Sizzle went the sausage. Crack went the egg. An English breakfast. Yes please, yummy!
- **R** unning, jumping, swimming and throwing. Amber is great at sport like a Championship Queen. Want to learn a new sport? Then go to Amber.

Bella Champion (10)
St Peter's Catholic Primary School, Waterlooville

The Bus To The Moon

I have always wanted,
To drive a bus,
All the way up to the moon,
But I am so very scared,
That my poor little bus,
Is going to simply go boom!

First of all,
I need a driver,
Where will I find one of them?
Oh look over there,
A tall-looking man,
He looks like his name is Ben.

So I've got a driver,
What else do I need?
Oh yes, I need some food,
Oh look over there,
Some tasty treats,
That look like they can brighten my mood.

So off I go,
In my bus,
All the way up to the moon!
Don't worry,
I won't be long,
I will see you soon.

This is a dream,
Everyone has them,
But they can be scary too,
What will your next dream be?
Will it be red
Or blue?

Amelia Knight (10)
St Peter's Catholic Primary School, Waterlooville

A Kitten's Dream

A kitten's dream,
Once strong and wild,
Wishing to go to space,
He dreamt,
And dreamt,
And dreamt,
Until *poof* - a rapid rocket appeared,
Like the magic that lingered in the air,
But now he needed to pack,
He needed a crew and some food,
So off he went,
Destined to accomplish his dream,
Oh no,
He forgot his water,
So the aliens found some,
And some new friends too,
They travelled space together,
They went to Mars and Jupiter,
And so they say,
They are still visiting planets today,
So follow your dreams,
Making friends,
Laughing and joking around,

And you could be like him,
Travelling through space,
With aliens.

Eve Jordan (9)
St Peter's Catholic Primary School, Waterlooville

Daisy And The Hedgehogs

There once was a girl who lived in a world
Where the skies were galaxies.
The stars sang and the hedgehogs danced
And pranced like a ballerina.

She lived in a house full of hedgehogs
Walls made of cotton candy
And a roof made of chocolate
And a rainbow door
And marshmallows on the floor
She danced and pranced all year round
In her little house with her little mouse.

The stars dripped and went bang.
She was as beautiful as a flower
And had lots of power.
Without her in the world,
There would be nothing.
Daisy loved hedgehogs
And all animals big or small.
Her twin would sing.
Daisy would dance in France,
Forever and evermore.

Bethany Stockman (9)
St Peter's Catholic Primary School, Waterlooville

My Dream Job

Honestly, I don't know what dream job I'd like.
An astronaut?
A milkman?
A pirate?
Wait, can you still be one?
Anyway, I still don't know,
I'd like to be an astronaut
But I have doubts about dying.
I don't want to be a policeman
Because I'd have to get rough.
I'd like to have a pet dragon
But they don't exist.
I don't like football
If that helps.
I play video games
And I like to think
I'd be an astronaut now
But I'm too young and
I'm doing this in school
So I don't have any more time.

Alexander Broadway (10)
St Peter's Catholic Primary School, Waterlooville

Amazing Dreams

A dream is your dream,
M arvellous or crazy,
A dventurous or great,
Z oos, cities, or castles, you choose,
I magination is in your hands,
N ow listen, dreams are like presents and treasure,
G o into your bed tonight and dream,

D reams are special,
R idiculous or just amazing,
E legant or marvellous,
A mazing dreams are from amazing imaginations,
M aybe your dream is to be on a bus on the moon, or animals, or a superhero; it could be anything you want,
S o dream on.

Temperance Parkes (10)
St Peter's Catholic Primary School, Waterlooville

Entering The Galaxy

S ecrets are still to be uncovered in the mystical galaxy of stars, planets and moons. Space is a long, beautiful void of pink, purple and blue,
P lanets of different magic and life, big or small, gas or ice, are all unique in their ways,
A ngry raging storms on the biggest gas giant in our solar system,
C ircling the sun, the eight planets, Venus is the hottest planet, Earth is the only planet with life,
E xciting adventures await us as we explore space and discover the wonders of our solar system, the Milky Way.

Sophia Lipscomb (10)
St Peter's Catholic Primary School, Waterlooville

Colourful, Funny Dreams

D iving into bed, colourful, funny dreams fill my head,
R aging rhinos, and dancing dinosaurs, they all come to play in my dreams,
E lephants fly to the moon using their super farts to zoom - *boom, boom, boom!*
A pricots dance, and cucumbers prance, they all do this in my dreams,
M oving, rolling in my pillows, I get a nightmare where I start to glow,
S haking me awake, my mother says, "Good morning." I wish I could do it again, instead of something boring!

Molly Nelson (9)
St Peter's Catholic Primary School, Waterlooville

Dreams Are True

Dancing and prancing, we soar high in the sky,
Away from the dream catcher, she eats dreams like a dragon over a boy scooter,
Me and a fairy called Amy and are only the last of us; we are,
The lonely unicorn starts to sing about going last as we are discovered by a lost soul,
My only fear is her now,
She is here, she falls and cries,
I am sorry, I really am,
I never knew you were so true, and I feel bad now,
I regret it now.

Makayla Williams (10)
St Peter's Catholic Primary School, Waterlooville

A World Of Dreams

A world of dreams although it seems strange
A world of dreams is all about things nobody knew
A world of dreams are things that can be made from me and you
A unicorn
An astronaut
A mystical creature in the tallest tower
As you dream of the longest flower
Close your eyes and dream some dreams...
A world of dreams
As you fall far from the real world like a bee from its nest
And you fall into a world of dreams.

Florence Turner (9)
St Peter's Catholic Primary School, Waterlooville

Funny Giraffes

In my land, giraffes lay eggs,
And everything else you wish for,
Giraffes are tall but also small,
Giraffes can talk, and best of all, they eat Weetabix,
The houses in my land are of all kinds of shapes,
There are portals, passageways and, well... everything!
All the animals are mostly giraffes and just giraffes,
In my world, giraffes are funny and lay eggs in
Weetabix bowls to keep the babies safe.

Catherine Cope (9)
St Peter's Catholic Primary School, Waterlooville

Unicorns' Magic Land

Unicorns go neigh as their horns change from colour to colour,
As their hooves gallop across the field,
The fairies flutter like snow,
The leaves fall for the fluffy, smooth, smiley unicorns to eat,
As the world tips like an earthquake,
The sky glitters like a rainbow as colours shoot from the grass,
The trees talk like a wooden plank,
Multicoloured flowers pop like a can of Coke.

Taylor Barnfield (9)
St Peter's Catholic Primary School, Waterlooville

Chocolate Poem

Chocolate is yummy,
Chocolate is fun,
Chocolate is silky,
Just like a bun!
I love chocolate, what about you?
Here are a few that I like too!
Chocolate cookies, chocolate ice cream,
Chocolate pudding, chocolate cakes,
Chocolate pies, chocolate nests,
Chocolate strawberries and chocolate icy shakes!
I love chocolate yum, yum, yum,
I love chocolate in my tum.

Fia Panamchickal (9)
St Peter's Catholic Primary School, Waterlooville

All About Football

Football, football
What a wonderful sport
You boot the ball
Oh, wait... it's in, *goal!*
Anyone can play football
Boys, girls, even adults.
You run the length of the pitch
Remember, don't be rude
Or your dream might not come true.
That's it for now but remember
Anyone can play football
It does not matter
If you are big, small or tall.

Hallie Puddick (10)
St Peter's Catholic Primary School, Waterlooville

The World I Live In

Whilst my teacher talks nonsense all day,
I dream of the world I live in today,
I spend my days in Jupiter,
I fly to the sun,
I go to Neverland,
Neverland of one,
With Pompey games every mile,
And one thousand kittycorns all called Kyle,
I eat chocolate all day and night,
But every day I discover all things new,
And hopefully one day I'll see you!

Maisie Hillier (10)
St Peter's Catholic Primary School, Waterlooville

The Unicorn

As she spread her wings to take off,
The sky lit up and the moon stood tall,
The unicorn spread her wings like a dove.
Her horn, as smooth as silk,
Magic as powerful as a sorcerer,
Her hair with strong and vibrant colours,
That is as bright as the rainbow.
She will always be with me!

Caitlin Nibigira (9)
St Peter's Catholic Primary School, Waterlooville

My Wonderful House

Once upon a dream, I thought about a house for me,
With hot chocolate water fountains,
Once I drank from it, it travelled down to my stomach,
As if it were trying to tickle my belly.

Once upon a dream, I thought about a house for me,
With toffee hanging on the ceiling,
Going drip, drip, drip,
Warm as a fire,
It sizzled as if it was trying to speak.

Once upon a dream, I thought of a house for me,
With a bright tall door,
Made of beautiful chocolate s'mores,
Looking down as if I were a dwarf,
When opened they went screech,
Like a child letting out a scream,

Once upon a dream, I thought about a house for me,
With chocolate-covered bricks,
Holding themselves in place,
When moved they went scrape,
Although they were delicious to taste,
It was like I was trying to bite into metal.

Kaydan Holland (11)
St Winefride's Catholic Primary School, Shepshed

Untitled

A rapper that has a shine of talent,
He releases his songs and gets on the mic,
He spits bars that he knows everyone will adore,
He knows he has the talent and the power,
Once, he sang from the Eiffel Tower.

He could be the best, and he could live a life without stress,
He knows he can; he knows he has lots of fans that love him,
I love his music and this new song,
But most of his songs are bangers,
He just has songs that don't go wrong.

He wants to be king, but everyone will vote for him,
That is the king,
He looked at his songs, and he said wow,
I didn't know I could do this kind of song,
Am I that good? He questioned himself.
How did I do this? I must be good,
Soon, he will have too much money that could flood his room,

He lives in a mansion, but not an ordinary one, he has a 500-inch TV,
He even has a pool that could be a water park.

He wants to make everyone happy and feel his music,
He wants everyone to choose it; he has relatable lyrics from when he was alive,
He already has five billion pounds in his bank,
He's got a nice flashy car that can drive far,
It goes too fast and is good with speed.

If he wanted, he could have the whole world to feed,
He rules the world and has power,
He even has a golden shower,
And that is his life.

Isaac Wasilewski (10)
St Winefride's Catholic Primary School, Shepshed

Once Upon A Dream

As the King of all Dragonkind, I have to have a palace,
A magnificent palace I do have.
My palace is a massive mansion of soft, fluffy cushions and marshmallows.
A hot chocolate fountain stands in the centre of an edible courtyard.
Kittens of every breed poke their cute, furry heads out of every window, gate and door.
The roof is a volcano full of pizza and fries.
When it erupts, it's raining food.
To top it off, a hard, sweet toffee door stands tall and strong at the entrance to my home.
This is my palace.

As I was taking a peaceful swim in my pool of melted white chocolate, I heard a rumble.
The volcano was erupting!
With a deafening bang, a whole twelve-inch pepperoni pizza flew out of the volcano.
Fries rained down on me.
A whole Domino's pizza meal was flying towards me.
It was heaven.

One day, on the way to my pool,
I saw one of my kittens walking up to me
On its hind legs with a cup of coffee.
"Good day, Sir," it said, "this is all a dream by the way."
And that was it.

Eric Turland (10)
St Winefride's Catholic Primary School, Shepshed

Unusual Dreams

Once upon a dream,
For once, I'm not staring at a screen,
Instead, I find myself in a land of green,
Surrounded by trees, with a lovely gentle breeze,
As I lie in the fallen leaves, like a resting cat,
I find myself drifting into extremely rough seas, crash!

Once upon a dream,
I'm not so at ease,
I spy eyes - pirate eyes,
As I'm forced to walk the plank,
I feel the need to scream, aargh!

Once upon a dream,
I'm now under the sea,
Hoping to find some buried treasure,
I stumble on a chest,
Filled with rich pearls and glittering gold coins,
Though I feel myself drift away.

Once upon a dream,
I'm floating in space,
Like a lost planet,
Passing by the beautiful shimmering stars,

Relaxing and carefree,
My eyelids become heavy,
And I begin to fall asleep.

Once upon a dream,
Finally, I'm in my bed,
What a crazy adventure I had,
I wonder what I'll dream about next time I go to sleep?

Freya Dunmore (11)
St Winefride's Catholic Primary School, Shepshed

Football Hero

Walking out of the tunnel nervously,
Butterflies somersault in my stomach,
As the roar of the excited crowds,
Scream my name,
Sounding like a million exploding fireworks.

The twinkling stars clapped us out,
As they shone brightly, brighter than the floodlights,
An explosion of colour filled the stadium,
The beautiful light show went off,
As fast as a shooting star,
They waved from side to side,
Like ballerinas as they tiptoe across the stage,
Colours filled the night sky,
As they roamed across the world of dreams like wild animals.

Each step I trembled with nerves,
Whilst the stadium roared like a lion,
As big as ten T-rexes and futuristic flying cars,
With two hundred thousand seats,
This wonderful stadium hosts the best games.

Wooh!
The whistle was blown,
The best game in history began...

Henry Clarke (10)
St Winefride's Catholic Primary School, Shepshed

World Of Water

It's all water in Dreamland,
The sky is cloudless,
Blue below shines like a diamond,
Fish tickle the bottom of feet,
Swimming in the never-ending ocean.

Nothing to clutch on; the world is all water,
Waves bash and crash into each other,
Like boats roaming into rocks,
Water engulfs the sun like an ice cream on a hot sunny day.

It's a world full of water,
Where no land to be seen,
Sharks orbit the world coming back and forth,
Houses made of seashells,
And jagged rocks that glide across the ocean like a ghost,
Eels scrape legs like rough brushes of steel.

Fish whizz off running from the vigorous sharks,
Big fish gang jump small sprats,
Dolphins jump over clouds into the deep water,
Only to come back again.

Jinu Labadia (11)
St Winefride's Catholic Primary School, Shepshed

The Land Of The Nogs

In Nogtopia, Nogs roam free in the luscious, grassy plains.
They use their big, fluffy tails to rush and race through the towering trees in the vibrant jungle.

The pink dandelions sway and dance in the breeze like ballerinas.
In Nogtopia, the blazing sun hovers above the white, fluffy clouds.
The roar of thunder bellows and howls. Crash!

The Nogs' footsteps are as deafening as a rocket crashing into the moon.
Their eyes are as bright yellow as a bee and their teeth as large as a rabbit's.
Their noses as big as a pig's snout.

They stomp and scream everywhere they go.
When they walk, they cause tsunamis and earthquakes.
The Nogs' screech is so loud that it can be heard from a different planet.

Evan Saunders (10)
St Winefride's Catholic Primary School, Shepshed

Chocolate Galore

Imagine a world of chocolate galore,
And how many things there would be to explore.
The chocolate rabbits and chocolate sheep,
And the marshmallow beds are my favourite place to sleep.
Imagine a world with caramel fountains,
That wave to the mountains next door.
All of that chocolate, just out in the wild,
Surely there can't be anymore.
Imagine a world with chocolate chips for breakfast,
The joy of waking up to it every day.
A world with Hershey's TVs to watch your favourite show,
Everything is chocolate; it's not hard to know.
Imagine a world that is full of chocolate,
The fizz, the pop and the bang by the lake.
Which dances to the wavy Mars bar leaves,
You can eat everything you need.

Hannah Sherwood (10)
St Winefride's Catholic Primary School, Shepshed

Creatures Of Sonaria

In Dreamland, mystical life wanders,
Beauty blossoms all around,
Creatures that look as if they are aliens, act and think like people,
As light shines in the dark,
Creatures eat and dance,
As six-legged, blue horses prance through the magical land.

Through the midnight air,
The wind blows and swishes throughout the night,
As four-winged, tiny dragons fly through the night.

When the sun rises,
The creatures take a tiny sip from the crystal lake,
Shiny fish jump out of the water in excitement.

When giant hammerhead-shaped rhinos,
Roam above the food chain,
Sleep peacefully in the cosy, blue, grass blanket of the jungle.

Fergus Flynne (11)
St Winefride's Catholic Primary School, Shepshed

A Mythical Dream

A whole world of wonder,
Is coming true,
Of mythical creatures,
And marvels waiting to see you,
Glowing horizon,
And explosions of colour pop!
A whole castle,
Gleaming like gold on a faraway hill.

Unicorns, witches,
And lots of fun,
Dragons hopping from rocks,
And a galaxy of wonder for the sky,
Stars dancing proudly, showing their shine,
As beautiful as a rainbow,
Full of joyful times,
Sweet-smelling air fills all around.

Sparkling waterfalls,
And glistening shells,
Crystals on every rock,
Rabbits sunbathing by the emerald-coloured lake,
splash!

Any food or drink of your choice, slurp!
And the moon made of cheese is glowing bright white.

Mabel Hill (10)
St Winefride's Catholic Primary School, Shepshed

Cotton Candy Land

Once upon a dream, a dream full of wonder, a dream full of candy,
Houses that smell of cupcakes and a caramel wafer as a door,
The marshmallows covered in chocolate sauce,
With a scoop of mint chocolate chip ice cream,
On top with chocolate walls around it.

The soft quilt that is,
As soft as cotton candy on a stick,
Falls as slowly as a bundle of clothes.
As comfy as a bed that you sink into.

Cotton Candy Land full of fun and joy,
With lots of games to play and enjoy.
Cotton Candy Land full of fun things to do,
There is never time to delay or lose.

Fairies, fairies,
Oh, ever so tall,
Oh, ever so small.

Yami Ugorji (10)
St Winefride's Catholic Primary School, Shepshed

A Dream Day In Paris

Paris, the land of my dreams,
Mickey, Minnie, Belle and Goofy,
Clang, crash, splash!
The rides spin around like magical dwarves,
Their dresses sparkled while they turned and spun,
The amazing flavour mixing in my mouth,
Eating Mickey ice cream and cold slushies on hot days,
Filling my tummy with desserts, eating Disney pretzels,
While they crumble into pieces,
Waltzing into the Disney Castle,
My castle, my face in shock!
Wondering what to do,
There was so much to do,
There was a Disney makeover,
Turning you into a magical Princess or Prince Charming,
Parents getting sugary goodness cookies and biscuits,
Yum, yum, yum!

Nancie Robinson (11)
St Winefride's Catholic Primary School, Shepshed

Animals

A whole dream of an adventure is coming true,
All of the animals,
Waiting to see you,
Butterflies around the rainforest dance like ballerinas,
Filling the air with vibrant colour,
Beautiful birds twirl and tumble,
Snakes slither through spiky bushes,
Like screams of deadly water,
Ready to drown their prey in venom.

Hopping frogs trying to get to the spiky vines,
From the top of the tree full of parrots,
Crystal-clear waterfalls,
Drip down the beautiful river.

Sun glowing like burning fire,
Birds flapping their wings across the sky,
As the sun rising reflects on them.

Clara Wardle (10)
St Winefride's Catholic Primary School, Shepshed

Candyland

Imagine a world with no rules.
A world of fun.
A world where you can eat everything.
The roads are made of a deep brown chocolate,
And the clouds are cotton candy.
There are marshes made of mallow,
And the trees, swirly lollies.

Imagine a house made out of hard chocolate,
The windows made of toffee.
The roof is made out of caramel swirls,
And a liquorice swing on the front.

Imagine a sea of golden syrup,
The waves reaching out to get you
Like a mother hugging her child.
The sand is made of pure sugar,
With mini chocolate turtles crawling around.

Zara Bayley (11)
St Winefride's Catholic Primary School, Shepshed

Magical Land

Once upon a dream, I was lying in my bed glazed with boredom,
I heard a sound,
Whoosh!
It made me jump,
I got up from my rickety bed and opened the window,
Slid down my long zip line and climbed into the treehouse,
I opened the cupboard and slid down the slide,
Whee!
I landed with a thump,
Everything was a blur,
I woke in a dark scary cave,
Argh!
A dragon woke up beside me,
Roar!
Out of the cave were the woods,
I ran and ran,
Reaching the world's most beautiful waterfall,
I saw the most beautiful unicorn,
It was the best dream ever.

Daisy Wright (10)
St Winefride's Catholic Primary School, Shepshed

Dreamland

Floorboards creaked,
Light crawled out from beneath a blazing sun.
Unimaginable scents made their way upwards, like a hand ready to pull you in,
A spell ready to enchant.
Opening it up, I was whooshed into a world of pure imagination.

Falling from the sky,
I stared in awe and wonder at the world around me.
It was like no other.
The houses lay on crunchy, air-like grass,
Solid doors of toffee,
Windows of gummy bears, not glass,
With bricks made out of sugar cubes.
Roofs of chocolate buttons
And Flake chimneys.
I knew I was going to stay a while.

Casey Clare (11)
St Winefride's Catholic Primary School, Shepshed

Dream Land

A whole new world,
Full of majestic creatures
And no pesky teachers!
Glowing, the horizon exploding with vibrant colours
Hugged the magical castle.

Fluttering fairy wings shone
As fire wooshed from dragons' chomping mouths.
Witches zoomed on their brooms and
Beautiful unicorns danced and turned into sparkling pixie dust.

Shimmering, twinkling and glimmering princess dresses
Flowed in the blowing breeze.

Witches who lived in ditches
Gave the creatures stitches,
Their noses as towering as skyscrapers,
They looked wicked!

Coco-Marley Gray (11)
St Winefride's Catholic Primary School, Shepshed

My Kitten Mansion

My kitten mansion is the best of the best,
It didn't even need a test,
It was my dream of all dreams,
It often has a kitten football team.

As you make your way around to the back,
You'll find many kittens pleading for a snack.

In the centre of the huge hall,
There stands a giant hot chocolate fountain.

The kittens plead for hugs and strokes
The kittenfall is the best bit,
Not a waterfall, but a kittenfall.

My Pepsi fountain is where people go to drink,
I even have a chocolate roof.

Joshua Monk (11)
St Winefride's Catholic Primary School, Shepshed

Untitled

As the wind swayed the trees,
It blew my tent around like a carousel of green,
Birds chirping melodious tunes,
I woke up yawning as I opened my windswept tent,
I drank my cup of coffee to wake me up a little more,
The tree wearing a shiny green dress gave me a jolly wave,
I crept into the caramel-dripping trees,
Collecting firewood of snappy chocolate,
The leaves whooshing around in the energetic wind,
Attacking my tent,
As I walked further and further,
The wind shouted,
I found some firewood.

Lucas Routledge (10)
St Winefride's Catholic Primary School, Shepshed

Magic Box

Once upon a dream,
I found a box,
A box that's full of magic,
Able to teleport me wherever I wish.
Whenever I'm ready, I snap my fingers and off I go,
I don't have to pay,
I don't have to wait,
And I don't need a car!

Snap! Off I go to a village,
A village that has me in shock,
People that are as small as ants,
And my thumb is as big as the shops.
I didn't stay too long in Tiny Vill,
I got locked up in an instance,
I killed too many souls!

Evie Llewelyn (10)
St Winefride's Catholic Primary School, Shepshed

Football

The football is falling from the sky, slowly coming from way up high,
The crowd have been roaring for the ball to come down,
Whilst the players are sprinting on the ground,
CR7 headers it straight into the goal,
The crowd start cheering it's a goal, it's a goal, it's a goal!
The keeper flings it up from the back of the net
But he isn't very happy as it is raining so he gets wet!!
Football.

Lerell Williams-Farmer (11)
St Winefride's Catholic Primary School, Shepshed

Once Upon A Dream

In Dreamland, it's a world of wonder,
It's my world of wonder!
Treasure is on top of every fluffy cloud,
Like it's playing hide-and-seek.

Everything in Dreamland is upside down,
You have to climb everywhere you go,
You see children hanging on monkey bars,
Trying not to fall into the blazing sun,
Knowing that if they do they might fall on a solid cloud,
Or a plane swooping by.

Oscar Johnson (11)
St Winefride's Catholic Primary School, Shepshed

Rodent Rain

Sometimes when a rat falls asleep,
They like to go down holes so deep!
So here we are, with a rat in his slumber,
Where he dreams about being trapped in thunder...
There he is, in his dream!
Where he is left with confusion and in desperate need,
But still, he can't think very straight.
Everything around him seems to be in a drenched, dull state.
The rat is puzzled, out of all places, why here?
He feels the insanity coursing through his veins and fear.
He is trapped in a maze of his own mind,
Where he feels lost and can't seem to find his way.
The thunder is loud and the sky is dark,
But he knows it's not the weather, it's the horror in his heart.
He hears the boom of the storms,
And sees the pressure up in the swarms.
A figure of few,
Coming down from the great, vast blue.
He looks up close, and to his surprise,
There are rodents raining down from the skies!

The little mammal is startled, he can't believe what he's witnessing!
The rodents get scattered around by the hefty breeze.
The atmosphere feels unusually wrong,
There's something out there that hums a song.
With no clear direction, they feel out of place,
His mind has been poisoned by the chaos in the space.
He looks everywhere for a way to escape,
But the clouds are blocking the moonscape.
As the growl of thunder enlarges, he feels more afraid,
The small-eared creature is lost in a dark void,
It seems that he has strayed.
His hopes of escape diminish with every passing second,
The rat is alone, yet he still reckons.
Rats and squirrels and capybaras fall,
Beavers, hamsters and guinea pigs crawl.
The crazed rat flees away.
It scurries here, it scurries there,
Trying to find its way through the labyrinth of rodents that drop like flies.
As it scampers all about, it runs and runs with trepidation in its eyes;
For it knows it must run fast or it'll meet it's demise.

When the critter awakes in a sudden panic,
He looks outside to see that it rains.
Drip, drip, drip.
Eva Kisyora (11) & Samantha
Stoneydown Park Primary School, London

Never Stop Dreaming

Dreams are the spice of life
They can take us to places we've never been
And show us things that we've never seen
In my dreams, sometimes I fly trucks and talk to ducks
It's an experience that feeds my imagination.

But not all dreams are pleasant
Sometimes my nightmares are filled with scary
Titans and hairy bison
They make me feel like I'm lost in a dark forest

That's why I cherish my dreams
No matter what form they take
Dreams give us hope
They inspire us to do better and be better

Without dreams, life is like
A broken-winged bird that cannot fly
We must hold on to them tightly
For if we let go life becomes a barren field

Never stop dreaming
Embrace your dreams
No matter how silly or strange they seem
They are the key to a happy, fulfilling life.

Jamie Bertram (10)
Stoneydown Park Primary School, London

Dream Off, Into Space

The moment your head reaches the pillow
The moment your eyes are fully closed
You know anything is possible
Just dream
You realise becoming anything
Becomes easy
There are limitless limits
Fly into a life you never imagined was possible
Or into what you thought was just out of reach
Fly into a life you want
Discover a new you
Reach into your dream.

Float into space
Drift into an endless galaxy of stars
See your home from a new perspective
Reach for the stars
Discover new planets
Dive into black holes that can transport you anywhere
A world where you rule.
Find out what no one else knows
Go beyond the limits

Drift off to space and go up
Drift off your bed and go up
Drift into space
Let your imagination soar off into the depths of space
Touch the clouds
Dream! Imagine! Create!
After all, anything is possible
Walk through your fears, through your doubts
Do what you want to

Become speechless, mesmerised, weightless, as wild as
a lion
Become you, an astronaut
Discover new theories and new lives
Swim through a sea of stars
Experience new feelings
After all, anything is possible, even going to space
Breaking the barriers you've always had
Go for your goal, your dream!

Wake up, wake up
The moment you realise it was just a dream
Just a dream
It hits you - it was just a dream
A dream telling you you can do anything!

Jasmia Lillie Kaur Marsh (9)
Stoneydown Park Primary School, London

Have You Had A Dream?

Have you ever had a dream?
I'd be stunned if you have not
Dreams are the most amazing things
I bet you can recall at least one that you have caught!

Dreams are very varying things
At night or at midday
Some will let you fly on open wings
But some will take you the other way

Have you had a dream at midnight,
Filled with monsters and fear?
A dream that made you shriek with fright?
Maybe even shed a tear?

Have you had a dream at lunchtime
About your ambitions and fantasies?
With fame, magic or something else
Where your imagination can take to sea?

Have you had a dream in the early night
Lying in your bed?
Here, the future's yet to happen
Pave pathways in your head

I bet you've read about a dream
From Shakespeare or J.K. Rowling
Where characters play comedy
Or hooded figures howling

I've mentioned lots of types of dreams
At many times of the day
The ones that make you want to scream
Or the ones that make you sway

So I do hope you enjoy your dreams
And treat them with respect
They really are exciting things
You never know what happens next!

Una Miller (9)
Stoneydown Park Primary School, London

Social Anxiety

You look around.
There are many people, and you feel your heart pound.
All of a sudden it all stops, there's nothing but a cold silence
That wraps around you like a blanket of darkness.
Just then, your world drops.
You're falling and you're drowning
You try calling, but it doesn't work.
Tears fill your eyes as you sink into the murk.

That's when you see them
Two girls that you had seen in the crowd
They sneer and laugh aloud
You feel an anger bubbling and you want to scream and strangle them
But you can't. You can't reach them.
It's as if they're floating further and further away
But the judgement is still as obvious.

Your insides are churning
And your patience, burning.
You squeeze your eyes shut and clasp your hands over your ears
To muffle the spiteful comments and remarks.

You open your eyes
It dawns on you that it was just a stupid dream
Just a stupid, stupid dream.

Arianna Laskou Fabrizi (11)
Stoneydown Park Primary School, London

My Once Upon A Dream

When I go to sleep, I dream.
I dream about you,
I dream about me,
I dream about surfing in the sea.

I dream about travelling to the big upside down,
If only I had a gazillion pounds!

Melbourne, Sydney, Byron, Perth,
I would visit everywhere on the Australian earth!

But for now, I'm ten, so I dream and doodle,
I'm inspired by magazines, I search on Google.

When I close my eyes, I fly, sail and glide,
I get so excited, I get giddy inside.

In my dream, I bungee, I ride, I canoe,
I wish that my dreamy adventure comes true.

It's been a long, long journey and I'm making new friends,
Then suddenly, Mum wakes me and for now my dream ends.

Once upon a dream, the world's upside down,
I *will* make it happen, I'll make dollars from pounds.

Ruby Swift (10)
Stoneydown Park Primary School, London

Sometimes I Dream...

Sometimes, I dream the extreme,
Sometimes, I dream the boring,
But I know I sleep deep,
Because apparently, I keep snoring.

I remember one time when I was sleeping,
One hundred percent, I wasn't peeping,
About a small elephant and a giant mouse,
The mouse was the size of an average house.

Once, I dreamed about chocolate buttons,
Falling out of the sky.
I also dreamed about being a blue whale,
Who has the power to fly.

Once, I dreamed about a tiny door,
That I had never seen before.
Near the sofa where I'm always sitting,
And inside, there were some trolls knitting.

Sometimes, I dream about the future,
Sometimes, I dream about the past,
But I know my dreams are the longest,
Because I always wake up last.

Alex Jeffery (8)
Stoneydown Park Primary School, London

Oh Midnight Sky

Under the canopy, oh so high
There I am, not knowing where to go
The midnight sky, a mesmerising sight
Where stars like jewels twinkle and sigh
Inviting dreams to take flight.

Still nowhere to go
Like a cosmic canvas, painted with care

I begin to walk further
Guiding lost souls towards hope's delight
Moon, a silvery guardian, casting its beam
Bathing the world in a magical glow

'What's that?' I think
A velvet cloak embracing the universe
Marvellous, not the midnight sky's grand looks
For its beauty lies in its infinite span
So when night falls, and you raise your eye
Look up, my friend, and let your spirits fly
The midnight sky sings, may you never deny.

Aleen Suleman (11)
Stoneydown Park Primary School, London

The Football Dream

Dreams are nice, unlike mice
I enjoy football, I enjoy games,
The thing I enjoy the most is getting hit in the face
I score a goal, don't just smirk, you have to work
Don't play for the trophy
But for the love of the game
It has little to do with the crowd
And has everything to do with the desire
To give everything I have to the game
Football is the best because no one wants to play anything else
Once you are a fan, you will understand the claim
Football is a way of life
Is a passion you can't just tame
It is good to work with your team
So you can win a game
You might be good
And you might win more games
Football season is here
One of the best moments of the year.

Arsema Yohhannes (10)
Stoneydown Park Primary School, London

Dreams Have No Limits

D reams make me feel like a superhero,
R oyal, like a queen,
E verywhere I turn,
A new possibility.
M ountains that pierce the sky,
S eas that never end.

H ello, I say to this new world,
A landscape of green and blue,
V iolet is the colour of the sky,
E verlasting forests of wise willow trees.

N asty branches with entwined limbs,
O r piercing eyes everywhere I turn, no! Not today!

L ight I always find,
I f darkness finds me, I leave it behind.
M e, mighty me!
I am the hero of this story.
T his poem has ended,
S o, I shall say my goodbyes.

Juno Scaife Duff (10)
Stoneydown Park Primary School, London

A Teardrop From The Galaxy

As I float into my world of dreams
I look up at my sky of wonders
and I see a teardrop from the galaxy.
I look down into the puddle of evolution
and I see two beautiful horses.
One that is white and black
and the other one is an amazing chestnut colour.
They are gazing up to the clear blue sky
with a rumble of the tractor in the distance.
Now in my dreams, I'm riding,
and all of my worries float away.
With a *clip clop*
my imaginary horse is trotting with me.
My horse is like a mind reader
and he tells me that he will only panic if I do.
Then I feel safe in the saddle.
Suddenly, he clumsily steps into the puddle.
Boom. My dream is over.

Lola Theophanous Richards (10)
Stoneydown Park Primary School, London

The Palestinian Dream

Full of hope with no home,
Dreaming to see the beautiful green,
Family passing with no silence.

The children of Palestine,
Their dreams are so pure,
And taken away by a world so unsure.

Their dreams of playing in peace,
Where olive trees and flowers could be seen
Running freely without fear
A world where peace is not near.

Their little dreams to laugh and live,
Every little girl and boy,
The dream of a home and school,
Learning all the golden rules.

Let us pray for Palestine,
And the children's dreams, so tender and mild,
That one day may come soon,
When peace will enter, replacing bad.

Hareem Shazad (10)
Stoneydown Park Primary School, London

Dreaming

D reaming in the night, where the moon is nice and bright.
R unning like a flash, to see a star crash.
E ager eyes looking left and right, looking for its shining light.
A mazed by seeing it dazzle in the night, feeling like we both have something in common.
M ounting its back up, up in the sky, seeing fluffy clouds waving hi and bye.
I nspiration engulfing us as we fly over trees, mountains, rivers and seas.
N eon lights flickering in the night, a memory that will stay forever in our minds.
G reat things happen if you dream big, so just close your eyes and let yourself be carried by your inner light.

Delia Danciu (10)
Stoneydown Park Primary School, London

A Dream Of The Night Sky

What ink is better to tell a story
Than the dark of the night sky?
Seeped in bright and shining glory
The stars above shine so high.

A symphony of colour
Pulses through the dark
The sky could not be fuller
Of tiny pinprick marks.

A shooting star races by
Fizzing with delight
I am in awe of the way it flies
And soars through the night.

I'm floating on a cloud so light
Made of moonlight bright
Watching stardust on its flight
The night sky seems just right.

I feel the softness envelop me
I open my eyes to see
I am at home in bed
I smile and lay back my head.

Robin Coffey (10)
Stoneydown Park Primary School, London

The Dream

My dream when I wake up
Is the dream to be seen
My dream when I turn up
Is the dream to be free
The dream of tomorrow
Which is happening to me
Is the dream to continue
Is as happy as can be.

My dream is a place
Of a land that's all fair
A place I belong to
A place that's not rare
A feeling of comfort and a feeling of care
The message to continue
The dream everywhere
It's fair, oh yeah!

My dream when I wake up
Is the dream to be seen
Buried in my heart
Always there as a theme
This is my dream
And this dream is just me.

Leo Michael Hoyle Buryy (8)
Stoneydown Park Primary School, London

That's The Dream For Me

It's supposed to be every little girl's dream to be a queen
Locked in a castle for eternity
To rule the world her majesty
But that's not the dream for me
The dream that I desire is a dream that inspires
That's the dream for me
To be up in the stars staring at Mars
That's the dream for me
To float in the galaxy with no gravity
That's the dream for me
The dream that I desire is a dream that is denied
So to all those little girls who think they have to hide
Hold on to your dream and say it with pride
Dreams aren't just dreams, they are who you are inside.

Eila Danaher (11)
Stoneydown Park Primary School, London

My Dream!

My dream when I wake up,
Is the dream to be seen.
My dream when I turn up,
Is the dream to be free.
The dream of tomorrow,
Which is happening to me.
Is the dream to continue,
Is as happy as can be.
My dream is a place of a land that's all fair,
A place I belong to, a place that's not rare.
A feeling of comfort and feeling of care,
The message to continue,
The dream everywhere.

It's fair! It's fair!

This is my dream,
The dream of comfort,
With careness and kindness,
Which exists in here.

The place of fairness!

Teddy Buryy (9)
Stoneydown Park Primary School, London

Dream World

Dreams, dreams, an interesting sort
You could be anywhere, fields or a fort
You could have nightmares in deep dark lairs
Or hissing dragons with menacing glares
You could have dreams about candy fields
Or daring knights with glimmering shields
You could be flying up in the air
Looking down at the houses there
You could have realistic dreams with your friends
Or be on a boat that never ends
But then you wake up and start to yawn
And realise it's the break of dawn
You run downstairs and start to shout
The night adventures travelling about.

Zoë McClintock (8)
Stoneydown Park Primary School, London

Snap Out The Nightmare

Run, run as much as you can,
Tonight you haven't made a plan.
Raves spit poison, eagles swoop down,
To catch you as prey and take you to town.

Doors slam shut in front of you.
Quick, find another way to get through
Legs heavy, voice gone
Nightmare, nightmare take me elsewhere

Witches cackle, wizards chuckle
You're being attacked by the curse of blades
So you better evade.

Run through horrifying portals.
Run through haunted houses,
Even run through the void
But they will still
Catch you.

Soner Ramadan (9)
Stoneydown Park Primary School, London

The Journey Of The Windrush

(Inspired by John Agard's 'Windrush Child')

Behind you, Windrush child
Grandma's tears are the only sound
In front of you, Windrush child
Hope shall be found
Surrounding you, Windrush child
The seas swirling round and round
After a week, the horn announces the doors of a new beginning, opening wide
As I get off the ship cameras flicker from every side
And I leave my life in a distant tide
As I walk on the street I am met with disgusted eyes
And as usual, the government has been telling us lies
My life has been flowing like a stream
But I still have my dream.

Alisia Blaiu (11) & Lena Bak (11)
Stoneydown Park Primary School, London

What I Do At Night

As I close my eyes,
My wolf spirit will rise,
A world of my own,
Only me and my pack will roam,
As I run through the streets,
My pack brothers and sisters join me,
We enter the forest, it's deep waiting to be explored,
The ground is soft and damp beneath my pads,
Our fur brushes against one another,
As we stream through the ancient oaks,
The wolves behind me fan out like a cloak,
As we watch the starry skies disappear into the distance,
The sun starts to rise,
The night is over, but only until the next.

Roisin McTernan (10)
Stoneydown Park Primary School, London

The Spook

This month, I was hibernating
But I couldn't sleep
Because of a creep,
It kept nipping me.
I put my head under my pillow
And outside, I heard the rustling willow.
I cuddled my teddy
And asked if it was ready.
So we went outside
And saw a crow on its side
And it asked for a ride.
Flying over the fence,
We saw a bunny.
We called it Hopper,
Suddenly, it turned into a 'popper' dog
Suddenly, it turned into a monster
Then I woke up.
Phew, it was just a dream.

Iris Hobhouse (7)
Stoneydown Park Primary School, London

Dream Land

When I dream I disappear
I go far away and reappear

I go far away to my dreamland
Where birds will fly or give a helping hand

In this world I am free
In this world, I feel so much glee.

In this world nobody's formal
In this world nobody's normal

In this world, you can imagine
In this world, anything can happen,

When I wake up and I'm in bed
I still feel glee inside my head.

I know if I imagine.
I can make anything happen.

Nell Dyer (10)
Stoneydown Park Primary School, London

My Imagination

My imagination
Is my inspiration
Whatever it is.

It might be a dream house
It might be a friendly mouse
It might be your sis.

It might be pink rain
It might be a rainbow cane
As long as it makes you happy.

It might be something purple
It even might be a turtle
Not anything droopy.

As long as it's got no rizz
My imagination
Is my inspiration
Whatever it is.

And it's my dream
Don't spoil it with a whizz.

Janae Benjamin (10)
Stoneydown Park Primary School, London

The World Of Dreams

In this world, I see I can fly
I lift my feet and touch the sky.
In this world, I find me sitting on a throne,
Being carried by drones.
In this world, in my home,
I can see wild animals roam.
In this world, hand in hand I'd hunt for stars,
And lock them up in jam jars.
In this world, I would wear gloves
And all I see is my mother's love.
This is a world full of dreams
Which doesn't look real as it seems.
This is a world that makes the impossible, possible.

Fatima Sherazaye (7)
Stoneydown Park Primary School, London

Ocean Dreams

When I dream I dream of the sea and its beautiful scenery
Adventure, *splash*, I jump in, and open my eyes
A whole other world, all the colours of the rainbow
Whoosh, splash, a dolphin swoops me from under my feet
I can hear the waves crashing and bashing on the shore
I see sailors sailing on the deep blue
Fish jumping around me and my canoe
I wake up and think about my ocean dreams
I would one day like to go adventuring on the sea
But for now, keep dreaming.

Macy Matthews (10)
Stoneydown Park Primary School, London

Look Into The Eyes Of The Owl

Read me,
Face me,
And look into the eyes of the owl,
Just wisdom, faith and humankind,
But look into the eyes carefully around you,
Them looking at you everywhere steering and mapping your days,
And this is something my teacher told me,
Life isn't a straight line,
As you live that would one must be perfection,
And it goes through zig zags and mountains all the way through,
But now look at the eyes of the owl once more,
And observe how you belong!

Irene Mara Arroyo-Kalin (8)
Stoneydown Park Primary School, London

Up In The Clouds

Somewhere up there
Somewhere in your dreams
In your imagination, there will be
A place for you
A place for me
Mine's up in the clouds
Come with me and you will see
How lovely and fresh the
Arctic, clear air all around us could be
All you have to do
Is jump on a beech tree leaf
And come up, come up, come up
because I know there will be a place
For you and no one else will
Be able to create it
It's your own unique place.

Lara Hodgkin (7)
Stoneydown Park Primary School, London

World Of Colour

Last night I dreamt I drew a picture,
And I used:
Warm red for the cosy bed,
Cocky blue for the sticky glue,
Bright green for the broccoli ice cream,
Vibrant yellow for the yummy marshmallows,
Jet-black for the mischievous cat,
Crunchy grey for the horse's hay,
Pastel pink for the fearsome lynx,
Light purple for the baby's gurgle.
And pure white for the peaceful kites.
I woke up and wanted to colour in the whole wide world!

Flynn Bullett (7)
Stoneydown Park Primary School, London

Yummy Sponge Puddings

On the seat sat an empty box,
Had they been eaten by a fox?
But the sponge puddings ran to King's Cross
They paid money to get on Aeroflot and flew to a mosque
They prayed to their god, 'Rosk'.
Then they marched to the door but instead slid on the floor
When they got outside they got back inside
They each ate a treat and ate very neat
But at the very last second a person ate them
And he thought they were delicious.

Dylan Junhua Lim (8)
Stoneydown Park Primary School, London

Frightmares

I have nightmares, I have frightmares,
Monsters underneath my bed,
Run away from Scissor Head!
Paintings with moving eyes, ghosts of people you despise,
Are my eyes getting blurry?
Or is that man getting furry?
Is that a black cape I see?
I don't know what bit me,
That man's skin is peeling,
Is it fear that I'm feeling?
Yetis with seven heads,
Attacking children in their beds,
Goodnight! Ha, ha, ha.

Charlotte Lawrence (9)
Stoneydown Park Primary School, London

My Hamster: Humphrey

H umphrey is special and sweet.
U s all could love hamsters for who they are.
M ountains are never higher than you when you have a hamster.
P hones are not needed around Humphrey.
H amsters are wonders.
R ocks are never harder than you when you have a hamster.
E ver loving, ever fun, lots of cuddles for everyone.
Y ou all have different opinions on favourite pets, but mine are hamsters.

Rose Gulla Martinelli-Kinmonth (7)
Stoneydown Park Primary School, London

Music Box

A piano and a drum had a prolific mission
To get through the corridor with no suspicion.
"Let's get out of this horrid place!"
The thick rigid door opened and the flute escaped.

They went to the kitchen to save themselves.
One by one, they jumped on the drum,
But mysteriously, Abel saw his phone was missing
And saw the piano with it.

So he threw the cable
And the piano was gone.

Abel Shajahan (8)
Stoneydown Park Primary School, London

The World That I Visit At Night

When I close my eyes colours flood in,
A world of my own, away from my kin.

I do what I want,
I see what I like,
I visit this world at the darkness of night.

I can eat honeycomb,
As I watch animals roam,
In the world that I visit at night.

I can climb up some trees,
And scab up my knees,
But it won't hurt because this world is mine.

No blood is shed,
No tears will fall,
In the world that I visit at night,
In the world that I visit at night.

Ania Jenkins (11) & Nina Dall'Igna Kennedy (11)
Stoneydown Park Primary School, London

The Banana Poem

Bananas, bananas, I am counting them,
Bananas, bananas, I can see ten,
Bananas, bananas, dancing around the park,
Bananas, bananas, climbing a landmark,
Bananas, bananas, down low and up high,
Bananas, bananas, falling from the sky,
Bananas, bananas, in the centre of town,
Bananas, bananas, being juggled by a clown,
Bananas, bananas, as lively as they seem,
Bananas, bananas, they love a sleepy dream.

Elisa Parker (8)
Stoneydown Park Primary School, London

Dreams Can Be Bad

Dreams can be bad,
But last night one dream drove me mad!
A werewolf with eyedrops firing from lasers,
His minions holding onions and wearing short blazers.

Onion air stung my eyes,
In the hole was blackness,
So I turned away with fastness,
I was stuck...

Soon the sun rose,
I felt a tickle on my nose,
My eyes slowly opened to see,
A furry paw on top of me!

Isaac Knowles (9)
Stoneydown Park Primary School, London

You Still Dream

In one night
You all have a sight
Which is called a dream
It could make your mind beam
You still dream on a holiday
You still dream when your parents are away
But if you can't sleep
I suggest counting sheep
And my dream is about when would I get sick
Or when would my team get a penalty kick?
And my dream is when would the world end
And how do messages get sent?

Murphy Hyland (8)
Stoneydown Park Primary School, London

Fairy Queen

Your dream is only your dream and no one can steal it
Imagination is your creation
If you don't use it, you will lose it
The fairy queen can affect your sweet dream
When the fairy queen is seen
She can be quite mean
So better to be still
Unless you're quite ill
As the sun begins to rise
You can open your eyes
Because it's all been just a dream.

Lily Kidby (9)
Stoneydown Park Primary School, London

Dreamland

I once had a dream
About a stream
It was a Dreamland
There was a band
Around it, there was sand
I stayed in a hotel for a day
In May
I ate a hash brown
I kind of frowned
It was delicious
Then I turned suspicious
I wasn't meant to eat it
Then I felt a nit
It was painful
I said it was rainfall
By accident
This is Dreamland!

Olivia Henrichfreise (8)
Stoneydown Park Primary School, London

A Magical Dream

Stars shine bright,
It's the magical light.
The clock strikes midnight,
And the carnival is awoken by moonlight.

Magicians have colourful canes,
They dance down cherry lanes.
Dancers twist and turn,
As children watch and learn.

Fancy top hats,
Dark purple mats.
This is all a dream,
It comes and goes like a stream.

Lena Bak (10)
Stoneydown Park Primary School, London

Dreams Of A New World

I go upstairs and get into bed
I fall asleep and block out the thoughts in my head
I enter a new world
With glitter and swirls
I walk and walk
And find animals that talk
What a wonderful dream
Where everything is nice
And you can go skating on slippery ice
But all the fun ends
When you turn a bend
Back into the abyss of sleep.

Mae Milner-Feliho (10)
Stoneydown Park Primary School, London

Teachers: I Make Sure

I make sure you are happy,
I make sure you have fun,
I make sure you learn new things,
I make sure people are treated fairly,
I make sure you live your best life,
I make sure you are nice to other people,
I make sure you are listened to,
I make sure you aren't hurt,
I make sure the school gets money,
I make sure everything happens!

Yaswinthan Pirabakaran (7)
Stoneydown Park Primary School, London

The Daunting Dream

Nightmares, nightmares,
Chase me away,
But they disappear,
At the break of day,
Cackling witches,
Pits of despair,
Hideous monsters,
In deep, dark lairs,
I run, I hide,
I shake in fear,
As I hear their footsteps,
Coming near,
Then I wake up
And start to scream,
Before I realise,
It was just a dream.

Amelie Dhoot (9)
Stoneydown Park Primary School, London

Nothing

Nothing is nothing, you can't just do nothing
Because when you dream you can do whatever you desire
Jump on clouds, fly on top of fire,
But when you wake up you find no clouds or fire
You just find yourself a bowl of cereal on the table
But don't worry, the next night you dream and dream again
So be ready to be tucked in for bed.

Isabella-Naomi Olohigam Ochinyabo (8) & Naomi
Stoneydown Park Primary School, London

The Dream Garden

The garden is full of dreams, surprises with every step
Filled with a paradise of perfect pansies
And towers of tremendous tansies
They harbour dreams till dawn breaks
And every single one of them wakes
As the scattered silvias sway gently in the breeze
All the dreams are being dreamt and whispered through the trees.

Elizabeth Eisenstein (10)
Stoneydown Park Primary School, London

The Dreams

The sky dream:
Sky dream, sky dream,
Goodbye dream,
Sky dream, sky dream,
Too high dream,
Falling from the sky,
Goodbye.

The short dream
In my dream, I run,
I hide, I skip, I slide,
Thoughts in my dreams,
I'm as small as a mouse,
But in my house,
I'm home safe.

Elspeth Simonds-Gooding (8)
Stoneydown Park Primary School, London

Untitled

M esmerising life-like graphics
I nteresting timeline
N ever will you run out of things to do
E ducational but fun
C reativity is your hobby
R idiculously funny
A dventures and surprises
F un is the best
T eamwork makes the dream work.

Nathaniel Kyeremeh Peprah (11)
Stoneydown Park Primary School, London

My Dream Is Poetry

Trees have birds
And books have words.

Gorillas fight
And atoms unite.

Nocturnal are bats
And active are cats.

Buildings have height
And the sun is bright.

And, if you get your abilities right
You'll become famous one night.

Dylan Roe (8)
Stoneydown Park Primary School, London

Falling

Falling.
Arms flailing and flapping.
Plummeting down as fast as lightning.
Whirling round looking down at the dizzying drop.
Falling.
Air rushing past.
Birds looking surprised as you drop past.
Thud!
You sit up in your bed panting.

Griffith Kingwell (10)
Stoneydown Park Primary School, London

Dreams Sweet Dreams

When the sky darkens and you go to bed
You know that you can dream big.
Drift off into your dreams -
Dreams are movies in your head.
Dreams can be exciting, funny, gruesome or anything in-between.
But they are mostly nice, sweet dreams!

Jaiyan Harrie Marsh (8)
Stoneydown Park Primary School, London

Art

I love art.
I do art because it's a huge part of my heart.
I like painting.
I like sketching.
I like drawing.
It calms me, it excites me and makes me feel happy.
The hardest part is knowing where to start.

Olive Bowyer (8)
Stoneydown Park Primary School, London

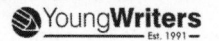

In My Dream

When I'm alive, I love to dive
Into a dream where it seems
I can fly high above just like a dove
Over hills, over trees, over mountains, over seas,
When I wake up, I'm sad because my dream wasn't bad.

Zara O'Neill (9) & Nina Hobhouse (9)
Stoneydown Park Primary School, London

The Moon, My Friend

Round and white
Big and bright
I see your face
The moon is my happy place
You live in space
So far away
Shine down on us
Every day
I wouldn't have it any other way.

Lennie Bradley (9)
Stoneydown Park Primary School, London

Cat

C ats are cute
A cat wore sunglasses
T he cat went on holiday.

Iris Simonds-Gooding (10)
Stoneydown Park Primary School, London

Cabbages (A Dream)

I like cabbages,
They're so cool,
I sit by them,
And drool.

Ivan Kennedy (9)
Stoneydown Park Primary School, London

YOUNG WRITERS INFORMATION

We hope you have enjoyed reading this book – and that you will continue to in the coming years.

If you're a young writer who enjoys reading and creative writing, or the parent of an enthusiastic poet or story writer, do visit our website **www.youngwriters.co.uk**. Here you will find free competitions, workshops and games, as well as recommended reads, a poetry glossary and our blog.

If you would like to order further copies of this book, or any of our other titles, then please give us a call or visit **www.youngwriters.co.uk**.

Young Writers
Remus House
Coltsfoot Drive
Peterborough
PE2 9BF
(01733) 890066
info@youngwriters.co.uk

- YoungWritersUK
- YoungWritersCW
- youngwriterscw
- youngwriterscw